THE CLASSIC GUIDE TO ALTERING PATTERNS

The Perfect Fit

Creative Publishing
international
Chanhassen, Minnesota

The Classic Guide to Altering Patterns

The Perfect Fit

Copyright © 2005
Creative Publishing international
18705 Lake Drive East
Chanhassen, MN 55317
1-800-328-3895
www.creativepub.com
All rights reserved.

**Creative Publishing
international**

President/CEO: Ken Fund
Vice President/Publisher: Linda Ball
Vice President/Retail Sales: Kevin Haas
Executive Editor: Alison Brown Cerier

THE PERFECT FIT

Created by: The Editors of Creative Publishing international

Managing Editor: Reneé Dignan
Project Director: Gail Devens
Art Director: Rebecca Gammelgaard
Writer: Peggy Bendel
Editors: Bernice Maehren, Susan Meyers
Sample Supervisor: Carol Neumann
Fabric Editor: Rita Opseth
Sewing Staff: Phyllis Galbraith, Betty Craig, Bridget Haugh, Kathleen Davis
  Ellingson, Wendy Fedie, Liz Hickerson, Jeanine Theroux
Photographers: Rex Irmen, Tony Kubat, John Lauenstein, Mette Nielsen,
  Albert Damon III
Production Manager: Jim Bindas
Assistant Production Manager: Julie Churchill
Production Staff: Michele Joy, Yelena Konrardy, Carol MacMall, Lisa Rosenthal,
  David Schelizche, Linda Schloegel, Cathleen Shannon, Jennie Smith,
  Bryan Trandem, Nik Wogstad
Consultants: LaVern Bell; Zoe Graul, the Singer Company; April Hollingsworth;
  Leah Peterson; Barbara Weiland O'Connell
Contributing Manufacturers: Ameritex; B. Blumenthal; Burlington Home Sewing
  Fabrics; Coats & Clark; Dan River Inc; Dritz Corporation; Dyno Merchandise
  Corporation; EZ International; Gladstone Fabrics, Inc.; Guilford Mills, Inc.;
  JHB International; Minnetonka Mills, Inc.; Moldex/Metric, Inc.; Pellon
  Corporation; Simplicity Pattern; Stacy Industries, Inc.; Streamline
  Industries, Inc.; Swiss-Metrosene, Inc.; The McCall Pattern Company; 3M;
  Vogue/Butterick Patterns; YLI Corporation
Color Separations: La Cromolito

Library of Congress Cataloging-in-Publication Data

The perfect fit : the classic guide to altering patterns / by the
editors of Creative Publishing International.
    p. cm.
ISBN 1-58923-227-5 (soft cover)
 1. Dressmaking–Patterns. 2. Tailoring–Patterns. 3. Clothing and
dress measurements. I. Creative Publishing International.
TT520.P447 2005
646.4'08–dc22

                          2005006395

Printed in China
10 9 8 7 6 5 4 3 2 1

Contents

How to Use This Book

Fitting skills are as important as sewing skills for creating garments of quality, value, and beauty. Yet, you can be an expert at fine sewing and not know how to fit. Perhaps you realize something is wrong with the way garments fit, but you do not know what to do about it; taking in a seam or two does not remedy the problem. Or maybe you are afraid of ruining a pattern by cutting it apart to make a fitting adjustment. *The Perfect Fit* helps you determine what steps to take and guides you through the fitting process so you can choose patterns and sew with confidence.

The Perfect Fit shows you the easy, practical methods for achieving good fit when working with commercial patterns. Using the fitting techniques in this book, you can change a mass-produced pattern sized for millions of women into a sewing blueprint sized to

The Four Steps to Good Fit

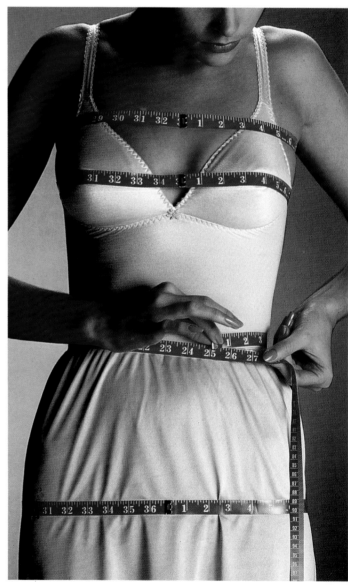

1) Analyze. Fitting begins with an exercise in self-awareness. Learn how and where your figure varies from standard pattern sizing. To make it easy to recognize your figure variations, we have provided a chart with more than two dozen photographs of common figure variations. The chart also tells how to select flattering pattern styles and how to avoid unflattering ones. After figure analysis, you know which pattern adjustments you are likely to require.

2) Measure. Accurate and objective measurements help you select the best pattern size, even if you fall between standard sizes. Four key measurements are all you need. This step takes minutes, but it can save you many hours. The right pattern size eliminates unnecessary pattern adjustments and shortens the entire fitting process. If you have had trouble fitting patterns previously, your solution might be as simple as choosing another size.

6

fit your figure alone. You can also make quick, minor garment alterations that make major improvements in the wearing comfort of the garment and flatter your figure.

To assemble the best collection of fitting methods, we consulted a number of experts. We asked professional dressmakers to explain how they fit patterns to their customers' various figure shapes and sizes and what it takes to create custom fit. We interviewed pattern company representatives for

information on sizing standards and patterns with built-in fitting help. We also polled professional dressmakers and sewing hobbyists to determine the most frequently made pattern adjustments.

We found that although fitting is a broad subject, it can be divided into four basic steps. *The Perfect Fit* shows how to take those four steps, so you, like the experts, can enjoy the benefits of good fit every time you sew.

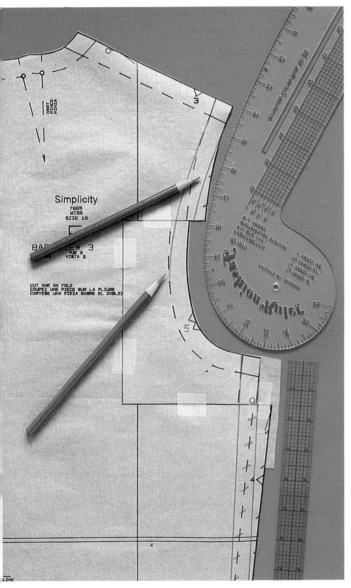

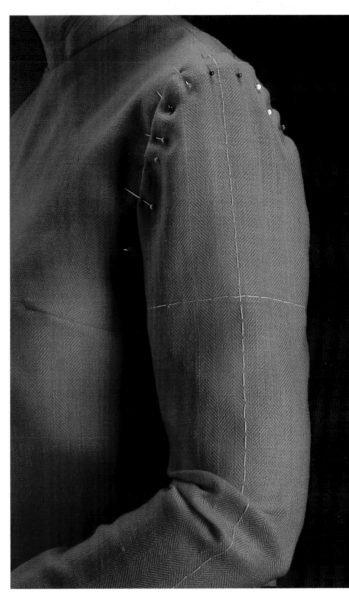

3) Adjust. Customize the pattern with major or minor adjustments before you cut. First make basic shortening and lengthening changes; then work from the top of the pattern down to adjust for body contour, posture, and bone structure. This section of the book is organized by figure area, such as hips and shoulders. In the photos, the adjustment line is red; the new stitching line, orange; and the new cutting line, blue.

4) Fine tune. Try on the garment as soon as the major seams have been sewn. This is the time to make minor fitting improvements. Steps such as adding shoulder pads, reshaping darts, and deepening the crotch seams can rescue garments that need help. By moving the buttons, raising a hem, or adding accessories, you can create optical illusions that help you look your best.

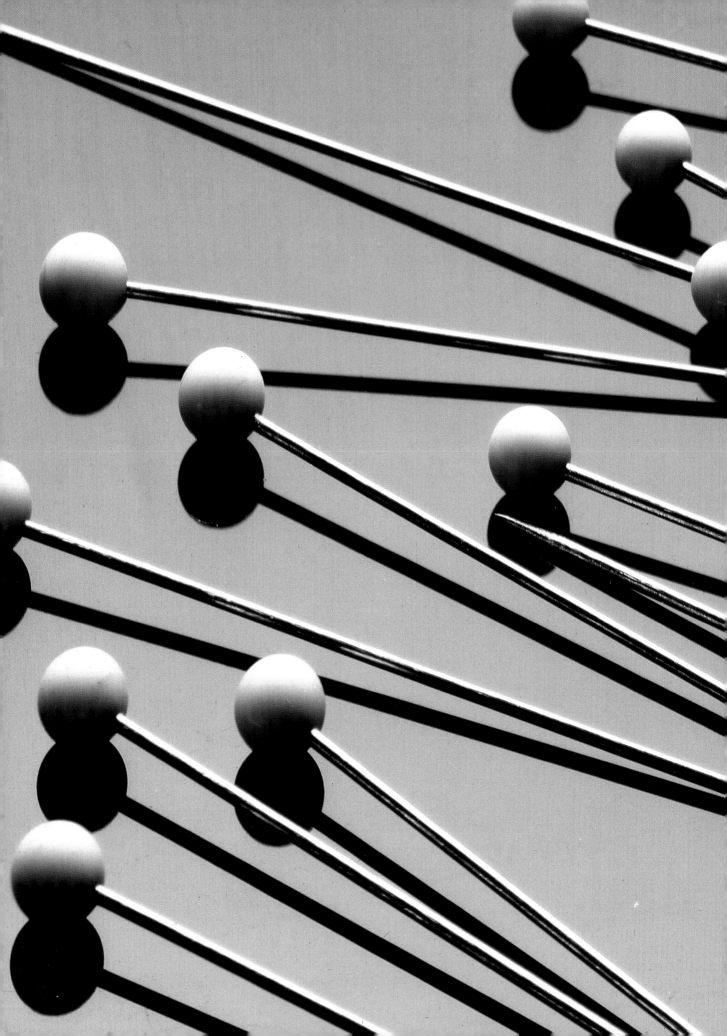

Introduction To Fitting

The Importance of Fit

Fitting is more than learning how to adjust patterns. It is achieving a feeling of self-confidence that comes from knowing that your clothes are comfortable and attractive. Well-fitted garments that are oversized look fashionably loose-fitting rather than baggy; garments that are close to the body allow you to move comfortably because they are not binding. Whatever the style, good fit eliminates unattractive wrinkles and gaping that draw attention to problems.

Fitting is more than following rules and calculating measurements. It involves judgment, understanding, and taste. Mastering the art of fitting is a cumulative process; expertise does not come instantly, but it does develop through experience. Some of that experience includes trial and error. When you have successfully completed fitting adjustments on one pattern, you can take similar steps with other patterns. In the process, you will educate your eye to see additional improvements worth making. Every time you work through a fitting technique you will learn something of value.

How Patterns Are Sized

The pattern industry uses a common set of basic figure measurements based on statistical averages compiled by the federal government for bust, waist, hips, back waist length, and height.

This industry-wide cooperation offers advantages for fitting. Although each company interprets these size standards in a slightly different way to make their patterns fit the greatest number of their customers, standard sizes allow you to purchase the same pattern size regardless of brand. This eliminates a lot of confusion, especially when compared with the sizing of ready-to-wear clothing. You might wear a size 14 in a name brand, a size 8 when a garment bears a designer label, and a size 16 in a discount brand. Because ready-to-wear does not always conform to pattern standards, do not select a pattern size according to the clothing size you purchase. It is purely coincidence if the two sizes are the same.

How Figures Vary

Patterns come in standard sizes, but figures vary. This does not mean you have figure flaws, just that there are differences between your figure and the commercial pattern. Pattern size standards do not define beauty or fashion ideals. They are simply averages. There are four ways that figures most often vary from those averages:

Length proportions of your figure may differ from pattern standards. Length proportions are where your bust, waist, and hips are in relation to your total height — something that varies greatly among individuals.

Contours (where and how much your figure curves) may differ from those on the pattern. Your bust cup and seat shape, for example, may not coincide with the average contour used for patterns. Body contours can change over time as you mature. They are also affected by diet, exercise, and undergarments.

Bone structure is personal, like contours and length proportions, and may vary from pattern standards. If you have narrow shoulders and a wide pelvis, for example, this bone structure will not change through diet and exercise. It is simply how you are built; however, it is possible to change patterns to fit bone structure.

Posture may differ from standard, average posture. Round shoulders and a swaybacked stance are posture variations. Posture is something that changes slowly with age, possibly becoming more exaggerated and leading to an unbalanced figure. Posture directly influences how garments hang, so you may have to modify your fitting methods to take posture changes into account.

Standards of Fit

As fashion changes, so do acceptable standards of good fit. Part of sewing well-fitted garments is being aware of the role fitting plays in fashion. Study fashion trends to interpret them in terms of fit. Then you can adapt fashions according to your preference and what looks best on your figure.

There are three basic types of fit: traditional, relaxed, and dramatic. Traditional fit is conservatively close to the body; relaxed fit is looser, more casual, and not as close to the body; and dramatic fit is exaggerated, generally very loosely fitted. Like fashion, fit follows cycles. At any time, one of these three types of fit will be more fashionable than the others, but you probably will find examples of all three in seasonal pattern catalogs and in your wardrobe.

A basic difference between these three types of fit is the amount of ease. Ease is extra room designed into a pattern or garment for comfort and style. The amount of ease varies from one fashion style to another and is often the key to how the fashion fits.

Ease can be adjusted, but avoid over-fitting by removing too much ease. Over-fitting destroys the fashion flair of a pattern. If you prefer close fit in garments, choose patterns that feature traditional fit. When using a pattern that features relaxed or dramatic fit, use good judgment to retain the right amount of ease.

Traditional Fit

Traditional fit closely follows the natural body shape. Conservative and classic fashion styles usually feature traditional fit. Examples include tailored jackets and blazers, straight skirts, dresses with waistline seams, tailored pants, jeans, and reefer coats.

Traditional fit is the most demanding, because patterns may have minimum ease for wearing comfort only — as little as 2" (5 cm) at the bust, 1" (2.5 cm) at the waist, and 3" (7.5 cm) at the hips. Occasionally, patterns allow even less. For example, wedding gowns and strapless dresses must fit so closely that patterns may include less than minimum ease allowances at the bust and waist. Patterns for two-way stretch knits may have negative ease; the pattern is smaller than figure measurements, so the garment stretches to fit.

These patterns leave little margin for error and require precise fitting, so traditional fit has the most specific guidelines for making judgments. Fitting checkpoints include the natural shoulders, bust, waist, and hips. On pants, the crotch seam and thigh area are also critical fitting areas. Sleeve and hem lengths are important as well.

Ten Areas of Fit

1) Neckline for classic jewel style rests smoothly on collarbone. Shirt band or Peter Pan collar can be buttoned comfortably.

2) Shoulder seams are straight across the top of the shoulder, ending at top of arm for classic set-in sleeves and sleeveless styles.

3) Sleeve caps curve smoothly around armholes. At elbow, dart or eased area falls at elbow when arm is slightly bent. The sleeve bends slightly forward below the elbow.

4) Sleeve hems or cuffs on blouse or dress end at wristbones when arms are slightly bent. Jacket sleeves allow ¼" to ½" (6 mm to 1.3 cm) of blouse or dress to show. Coat sleeves end ¼" to ½" (6 mm to 1.3 cm) below wristbones to cover blouse or dress sleeves.

5) Bust shaping falls at fullest part of bust and follows bust contours. Bust darts end 1" to 1½" (2.5 to 3.8 cm) from bust point for sizes up to size 14. For larger sizes, darts end 2" to 2½" (5 to 6.5 cm) from fullest point of bust.

6) Bodice back fits smoothly. Darts or shaped princess seams fit the garment to figure contours at shoulder blades and natural waist.

7) Waistline seam, lower edge of waistband, or waist shaping falls at natural waist. A skirt or pants waistband should have enough ease to fit your thumb between the band and your abdomen.

8) Back darts stop ½" to 1" (1.3 to 2.5 cm) short of fullest part of seat. Ease allows you to bend or sit down without straining the seams.

9) Seat and pants crotch seam follow your contours smoothly. Darts shape to contours without wrinkles, pulls, or dimples. Jacket hem falls above or below the fullest part of seat.

10) Hemline is equal distance from floor around garment. Avoid placing hem at fullest part of calves or thighs. Adjust hem for pants to touch top of shoe heel.

Relaxed Fit

Patterns with relaxed fit include design ease for a comfortable, loose fit. This is typical of casual sportswear such as windbreakers, culottes, jumpsuits, pull-on pants, and pullover tops. Other typical fashion styles include cardigan jackets; gathered, pleated, A-line, and wrap skirts; and trousers with front pleats.

Pattern details help define relaxed fit. Gathers, released pleats, wrap closures, elasticized waists and edges, and drawstring ties are easy to adjust. The waistline may be above or below the natural waist. Shoulder seams are not fitted to the natural shoulders for dolman, raglan, dropped shoulder, and some pouffed sleeves. Necklines such as scoop, bateau, and V-styles rest below the neck base.

Relaxed fit requires less precision than traditional fit. The most important fitting checkpoints are the neckline and the shoulders. The neckline should rest smoothly against the figure without gaping or wrinkling. If the garment has a convertible collar, it should rest neatly on the collarbone and upper chest without pulling toward the back or gaping outward. Dropped shoulder seams should fall forward of the natural shoulder line. Darts or shaping on raglan and dolman sleeves should follow the natural shoulder curve.

Sleeves should blouse gracefully along their entire length when the arm is slightly bent. Dolman sleeves should be in proportion to total figure; if necessary, remove excess from the underarm seam.

The bodice front of blouson styles should drape softly from the shoulders to the waistline seam, band, or ribbing. Extra length may be required for a blouson fit if the bust cup size is C or larger. Elasticized waistlines are sized to slide easily over the hips. Released pleats on skirts and pants should hang straight over the hips without being pulled open.

Dramatic Fit

Dramatic fit may not follow the natural body contours closely at all. Instead, the pattern may exaggerate figure shape for fashion emphasis. The pattern may add a peplum, for example, to broaden the hipline, or it may pad shoulders excessively to broaden the top of the silhouette. Dramatic fit includes garments that are loosely fitted throughout, such as caftans and kimonos; it also includes designer styles that feature elegant fabric draping, such as cowl necklines and surplice wraps. Evening wear often belongs in this fitting category.

You can recognize patterns that feature dramatic fit by looking at the general silhouette and the detailing. Pattern pieces with an unfamiliar shape also signal dramatic fit. Typical garments with dramatic fit include capes, harem pants, palazzo pants, peasant blouses, smocks, chemise dresses, bouffant dresses, and tent dresses.

Understanding how dramatic fit is supposed to look on your figure requires good judgment, a certain flair, and sometimes imagination. In many garments, the inner construction is crucial. To support the fashion fabric when the garment is shaped away from the body, you may need to use a specific shoulder pad or an interfacing of sufficient stiffness. To determine what the garment requires, study the pattern directions and suggested notions before you sew.

The shoulder area may be the only closely fitted part of the garment when a pattern features dramatic fit. If so, make sure the shoulder seams and neckline fit well as a good foundation for the entire garment. Check whether the fabric drapes on-grain throughout. If there is a cowl neckline or other draped detail, encourage graceful fabric folds by sewing weights inside. Below the shoulders and neckline, look for a fashionable flow of fabric. Some fabrics perform better if underlined.

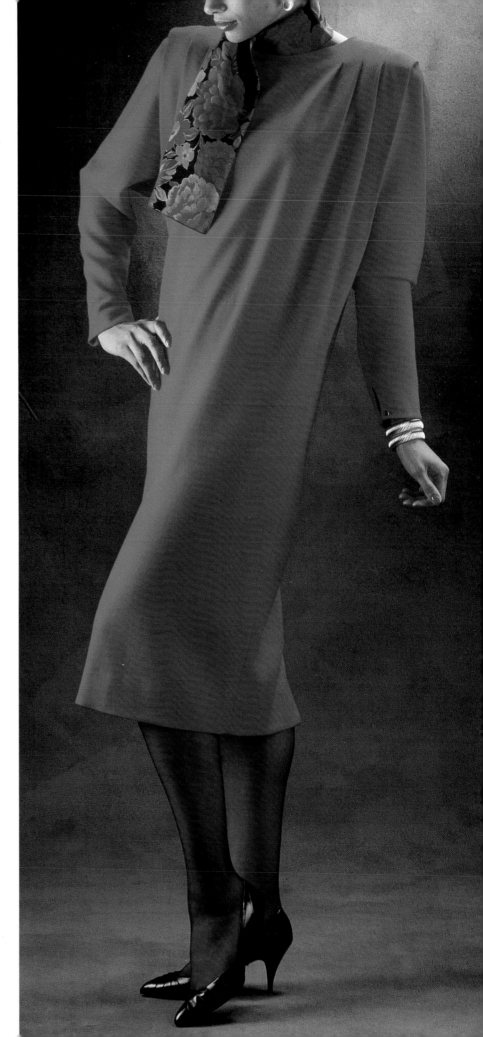

The Pattern As a Fitting Tool

Pattern companies recognize that a prime reason you sew is to achieve personalized fit, so they build fitting assistance into their products. The specific help in patterns varies from one brand to another; it also changes from time to time as companies develop new ways to address fitting concerns.

There are, however, similarities among the pattern brands. All provide fitting aids on the pattern envelope and on the tissue pieces. Some of this information is duplicated on the pages of the pattern catalog so you have it when making style selections; additional information is provided at the back of the catalog. These sources help you make good judgments and interpret fashion designs in terms of fit for your figure.

The Pattern Envelope Back

Line drawings show outline shape and design details of pattern, always from back view but sometimes from front view as well. See if darts or shaped seams bring fit close to figure, or if more relaxed fit is indicated by gathers or released pleats.

Descriptive caption furnishes style, fit, and construction information. Terms such as "closely fitted" or "fitted" indicate traditional fit with minimal ease. Terms such as "semi-fitted" or "loosely fitted" indicate relaxed fit with greater amount of ease. The term "very loosely fitted" indicates dramatic fit with generous amount of ease. The fitting term refers only to hipline for pants or skirt pattern, and only to bustline for a dress, blouse, jacket, or coat pattern. Caption also alerts you to fashion details that require nontraditional fit with terms such as "blouson bodice" or "dropped shoulder."

Finished garment measurements help determine key pattern adjustments. Width around lower edge of garment tells you amount of fullness at hemline. Finished length tells you how long finished garment will be. Compare finished garment measurements with existing garments in your wardrobe so you know exactly what to expect from pattern.

Size chart lists measurements for standard pattern sizes. Use chart as reference for comparison with your figure measurements to help identify need for pattern adjustments.

Notions list tells you whether pattern requires shoulder pads. If pads are listed, pattern has been designed with extra room in shoulder area to accommodate pad thickness. If you omit pads, garment may not fit properly.

The Pattern Envelope Front

Fashion illustration is drawn to strict specifications to reflect how garment looks when properly fitted. Study illustration to see drape of fabric, type of fit, and styling and accessory ideas. Sometimes a photograph is used instead of an illustration.

Label identifies patterns that include special fitting or size-related information. Label also explains whether a specific fabric, such as two-way stretch knit, is required. When pattern requires particular type of fabric, do not substitute another because pattern will not fit properly.

Views show options included in pattern. Use these options to create most flattering adaptation of pattern style for figure.

Size and figure type are printed at the top. If pattern includes three sizes, three cutting lines are printed on the tissue.

The Pattern Pieces

Dot, triangle, or square symbols mark joining points for adjacent garment sections. Often these are key fitting points as well. For example, symbol at center of sleeve cap on classic set-in sleeve lines up with end of your natural shoulders. Symbols label essential fitting checkpoints at shoulders, bust, waist, and hips.

Grainline arrow is essential reference for pattern adjustments. When you must draw your own adjustments lines on patterns, draw then parallel or at right angles to grainline.

Placement lines help you position pockets, buttonholes, and trims. You may prefer different placement, especially if you have made pattern adjustments.

Double line shows where to lengthen or shorten pattern before layout and cutting.

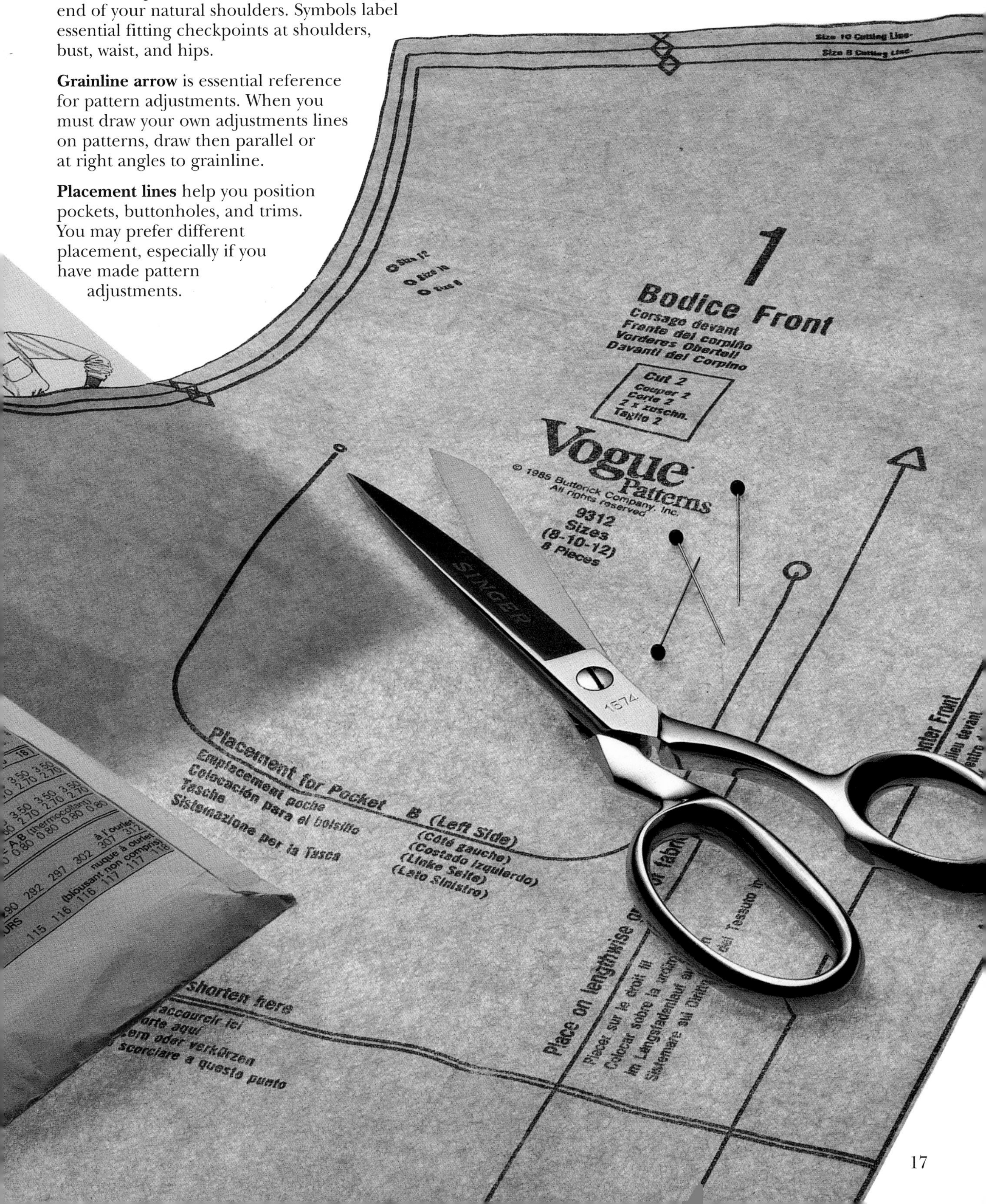

1

Bodice Front
Corsage devant
Frente del corpiño
Vorderes Oberteil
Davanti del Corpino

Cut 2
Couper 2
Corte 2
2 x zuschn.
Taglio 2

Vogue
Patterns

9312
Sizes
(8-10-12)
8 Pieces

Size 10 Cutting Line
Size 8 Cutting Line

Placement for Pocket B (Left Side)
Emplacement poche
Colocación para el bolsillo
Tasche
Sistemazione per la Tasca

(Côté gauche)
(Costado izquierdo)
(Linke Seite)
(Lato Sinistro)

shorten here
raccourcir ici
corte aqui
...em oder verkürzen
scorciare a questo punto

Place on lengthwise grain of fabric

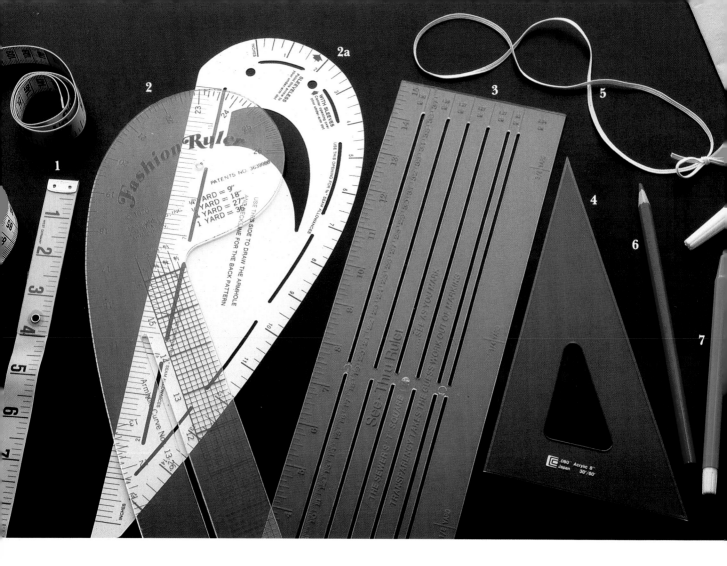

Fitting Tools, Supplies & Equipment

Fitting does not require many special tools or supplies. You probably have most of the essential tools of sewing — items such as pins, tape measure, mirror, rulers, tape, and paper. There are some other products to consider adding as you become more experienced at fitting. These products save time or make fitting easier.

One important essential is a helper. Ask a friend, dressmaker, or sewing instructor to lend a hand. Fitting alone is awkward, if not impossible. With help, figure measurements are more accurate and judgments are more objective.

1) Tape measure made from reinforced fiberglass or waterproof oilcloth is the most accurate. A tape measure with a 4" (10 cm) rigid plastic ruler at the end can be used as a short ruler and sewing gauge.

2) Curved ruler simplifies correcting curved stitching and cutting lines on patterns after adjustments have been made. Transparent type combines curved and straight edges. Opaque curved ruler (**2a**) has slots ⅝"

(1.5 cm) from the edge, making it easy to mark standard seam allowances.

3) Transparent ruler has slot openings spaced at convenient intervals for dressmaking, such as ⅝", ½" and ¼" (1.5 cm, 1.3 cm, and 6 mm). This makes it easy to mark parallel lines for pattern adjustments and to restore standard seam allowances. Use ruler corners as an L-square to ensure adjustments are at right angle to grainline.

4) Right angle triangle helps to locate cross grains on fabric, to square-off straight edges, and to mark adjustment lines on patterns.

5) Narrow elastic marks your waistline for figure measurements.

6) Pattern marking pencil will not smear or tear pattern tissue. Ordinary pencil can also be used with a light touch.

7) Washable marking pen or tailor's chalk (**7a**) is used for marking alterations on garments.

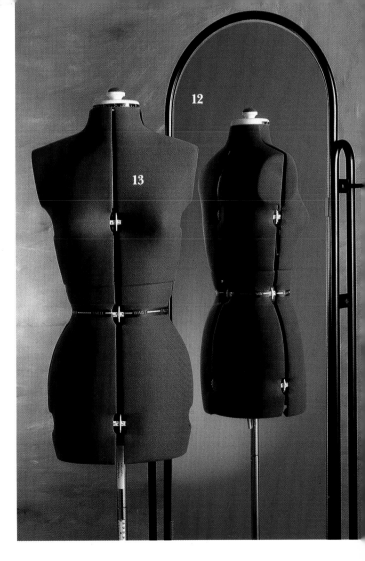

8) Peelable tape anchors pattern adjustments. Ordinary transparent or masking tape can be used, but peelable tape allows you to reposition pattern adjustment without tearing pattern tissue.

9) Extra paper is used to add to the size of a pattern piece during adjustments. Use gift wrap tissue, or recycle discarded patterns. Alternative materials include computer paper for major changes and adding machine or graph paper for minor changes.

10) Fusible nonwoven interfacing backs pattern pieces where clipping is required for pin-fitting, such as at necklines and armholes.

11) Trial fabric should approximate weight and hand of fashion fabric you will use for garment. Muslin **(11a)** is classic choice because it shows pulls and wrinkles clearly to indicate fitting problems. Woven gingham **(11b)** with checks ¼" (6 mm) or larger works well because the fabric design forms built-in grid for measuring amount of fitting adjustment required. Gingham also shows crosswise and lengthwise fabric grains clearly. Pattern tracing fabric **(11c)** is lightweight nonwoven fabric marked in a 1" (2.5 cm) grid. It is transparent enough to allow you to trace original pattern, and supple enough so you can sew the tracing as a test garment for fitting. Afterwards, remove the stitches and use test garment as your pattern.

12) Full-length mirror is essential throughout fitting process, from initial step of analyzing your figure to final step of fine-tuning the garment. Three-way mirror is ideal to see yourself from all angles without twisting.

13) Dress form is helpful for fitting when it duplicates your figure shape and contours as well as your bust, waist, and hip measurements. Use a dress form to pin-fit patterns, to check partly sewn garment for needed alterations, and to fine-tune details such as pocket placement and hemlines. Adjustable dress forms have dials to expand or contract isolated areas at bust, waist, and hips. Some adjustable forms also allow you to change neck circumference and back waist length. Another type consists of a foam rubber base, which is shaped to your figure by a fabric covering.

Understanding Your Figure

Analyzing Your Figure

The first step in fitting is understanding how your figure differs from the average figure that is used as a sizing standard for patterns. When you know where the differences are, you will know which areas of a pattern need adjustments to correct the fit. You will also know how to select pattern styles that flatter your figure and how to keep pattern adjustments to a minimum.

Be objective when comparing yourself with pattern averages. Everyone has figure assets as well as areas that need camouflaging. Avoid the tendency to dwell on your problems. Concentrate on your good points, and try to see yourself realistically so you can gain the most from the fitting process.

Remember, too, that it is natural for your figure to change over time. Do not think about how you used

How to Make a Figure Outline

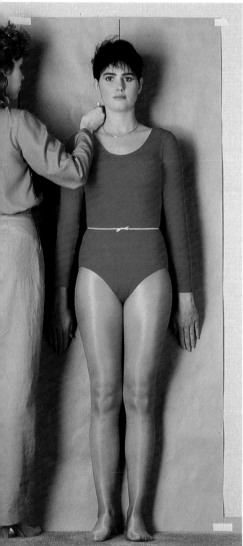 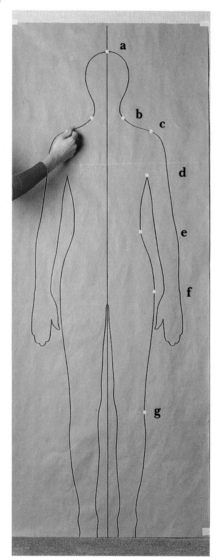 

1) Mount paper on smooth wall or door. Draw line through center from top to bottom. Stand centered on this line. Stand normally, with shoulders and arms relaxed and chin up. Ask helper to draw outline, holding pen straight and parallel to floor.

2) Mark top of head (**a**). Also mark right and left sides of outline at base of neck where necklace rests (**b**), ends of shoulders (**c**), underarms at creases (**d**), waist where cord is tied (**e**), fullest part of hips (**f**), and knees (**g**).

3) Use yardstick as straight edge to draw lines at top of head and across figure outline to connect marks at neck base, shoulders, underarms, waist, hips, and knees. These lines mark length proportions for figure analysis.

to look or about how you would like to look. Analyze your figure as it looks right now.

Making a Life-sized Figure Outline

To analyze your figure objectively, ask someone to help you trace a silhouette of your body. This outline is not a perfect replica of your body, but it shows your general figure shape and provides length proportion and figure contour guidelines. You can determine this information by studying your reflection in a mirror; however, with the drawing it is easier to make a more honest appraisal.

You will need a large piece of paper, felt-tipped pens, and a yardstick. Wear a loose-fitting leotard or bra and panties. Do not wear shoes. Tie a string or cord around your waist, and wear a short chain necklace around your neck.

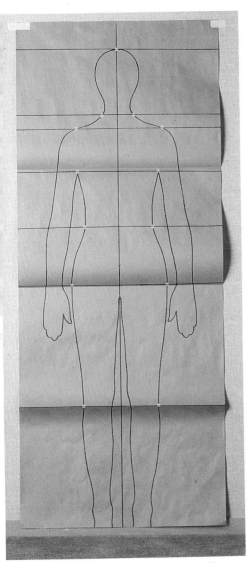
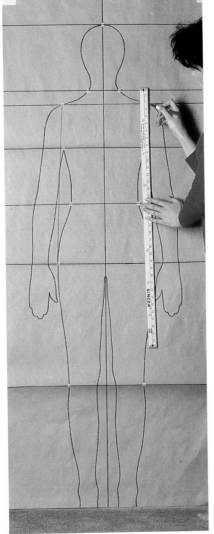
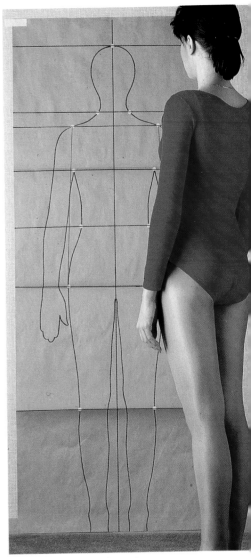

4) Remove drawing from wall. Fold drawing into fourths by folding in half with mark at top of head matching lower edge of paper. Fold in half again. Crease folds to show average length proportions for waist, hips, and knees.

5) Connect shoulder and hip marks on right and left sides of figure outline. Use second color of pen to emphasize these lines. They help you see your figure shape.

6) Stand back and squint to see outline as abstract shape. Analyze your figure shape as on page 26, your length proportions as on page 24, and your figure contours as on pages 28 to 32.

Analyzing Your Length Proportions

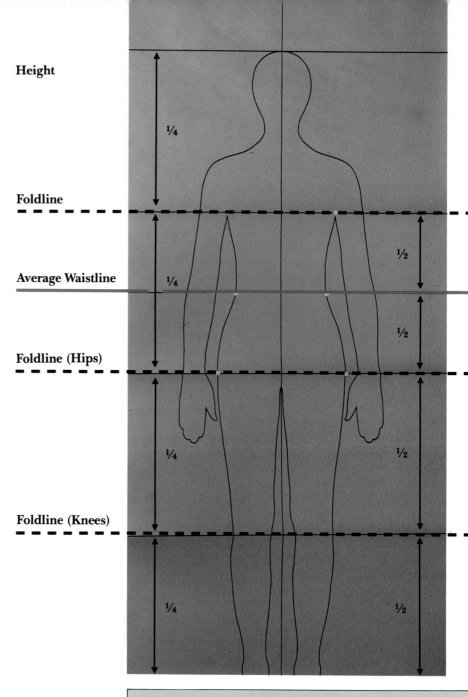

Height

Foldline

¼

½

Average Waistline

¼

½

Foldline (Hips)

¼

½

Foldline (Knees)

¼

½

To analyze your length proportions, compare the creases that divide your life-sized figure with the lines that mark your underarms, waist, hips, and knees. If the creases line up with the marked lines, your length proportions are average. If not, you are long-waisted or short-waisted compared with standard proportions.

If your figure varies from pattern standards in length proportions, select pattern styles that help balance the appearance of your figure. Design details such as waistline location and width can help you improve your appearance by disguising unbalanced figure proportions.

For good fit, shortening or lengthening adjustments may be needed at bodice back waist, hipline, crotch depth on pants, finished garment length (measured from waist to hem), and pants leg length.

Average Length Proportions

Figure is divided into four equal parts. Hips are at halfway point of total body height. Natural waistline is halfway between underarm and hips. Knees are halfway between hips and floor line.

Fitting goal	
Flattering pattern styles or details	
Unflattering pattern styles or details	
Common pattern adjustments	

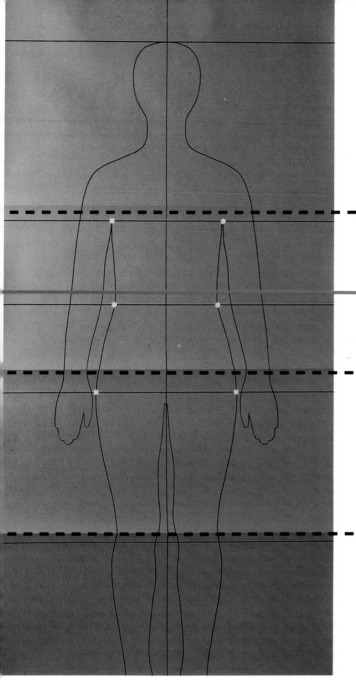
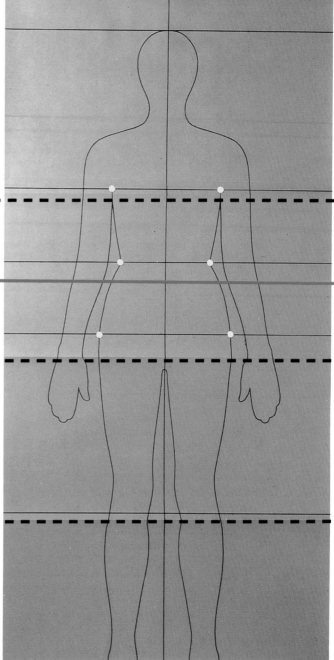

Long-waisted length proportions

Waist is *lower* than the average length proportions, or length from underarm to waist is *more* than half the distance from underarm to hip. Legs may be proportionately short.

Make upper torso appear shorter.

Wide waistbands, high-rise waistbands, raised waistlines, dropped waistlines with blousing, short jackets, relaxed fit above natural waist.

Body-hugging fit above natural waist, hip yokes, dropped waistlines with close midriff fit.

Lengthen pattern back waist length, lengthen pants crotch depth, shorten pants legs, shorten finished garment.

Short-waisted length proportions

Waist is *higher* than the average length proportions, or length from underarm to waist is *less* than half the distance from underarm to hip. Legs may be proportionately long.

Make upper torso appear longer.

Narrow or contoured waistbands, hip yokes, dropped waistlines, overblouses, tunics, long jackets, blousing at or below natural waist.

Wide waistbands and other waist-defining details, bodice-broadening details such as patch pockets, short jackets with hems at or above natural waist.

Shorten pattern back waist length, raise hipline, lengthen pants legs, lengthen finished garment length.

Analyzing Your Shape

Compare your figure outline with the average figure shape used as a pattern sizing standard. If your figure resembles the average shape, you will find a wide range of pattern silhouettes flattering.

Not everyone has an average figure outline. Three of the most common figure variations are shown at right. Choose the one that comes closest to describing your shape. Among the thousands of pattern styles available in seasonal pattern catalogs, there is something for everybody. Develop an eye for selecting the best styles for your figure shape, whether you like to keep up with current fashion trends or prefer to wear classics.

Tips for Selecting Flattering Patterns

Slenderize or lengthen figure shape by choosing patterns with vertical emphasis. Pressed pleats, vertical tucks, buttoned front closings, V-necklines, and princess seams accent the vertical.

Broaden or shorten figure shape by choosing patterns with strong horizontal emphasis. Yokes, wide waistbands, extended shoulders, bateau necklines, dropped waistlines, and Empire waistlines are pattern details that accent the horizontal.

Balance the pluses and minuses of your figure shape. For example, if the bottom portion of your figure looks larger than the top, choose patterns with details that broaden the top of your figure. As a result, your entire figure will look more balanced.

Minimize proportionately large areas by choosing patterns with little or no detail in those areas. If you want to camouflage a full bustline, for example, choose a pattern with plain bodice styling rather than a pattern featuring patch pockets across the bust or ruffles cascading down the front.

Accent attractive figure areas with patterns that have detailing in those areas. For example, a skirt pattern with a hip yoke or sarong draping shows off trim hips better than a plain straight skirt does.

Reveal figure shape by selecting patterns with traditional, close fit. Darts or contoured seaming in a pattern will show your figure shape clearly.

Conceal figure shape by selecting patterns with relaxed or dramatic fit, which emphasizes flow of fabric rather than the figure underneath.

Streamline fitting by selecting patterns with seams or other details in areas needing adjustments. Simple patterns that are easy to sew are not necessarily easy to fit. The more seams, darts, pleats, gathers, and other adjustable details in a figure area, the more opportunities you have to correct the fit without extensive changes to the pattern pieces.

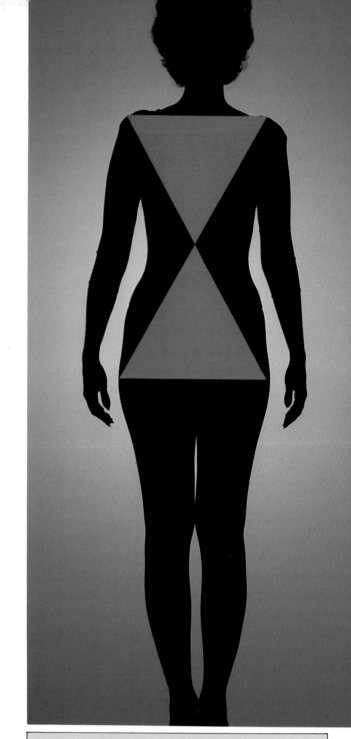

Shoulders & Hips Equally Wide; Narrow Waist

Average shape used as pattern sizing standard has shoulders and hips that look about equally wide, so figure looks balanced above and below waist. Waist is clearly indented. Pattern size charts use figure measurements to describe average figure shape — bust is 2" (5 cm) smaller than hips, and waist is 9½" to 10" (24 to 25.5 cm) smaller than hips.

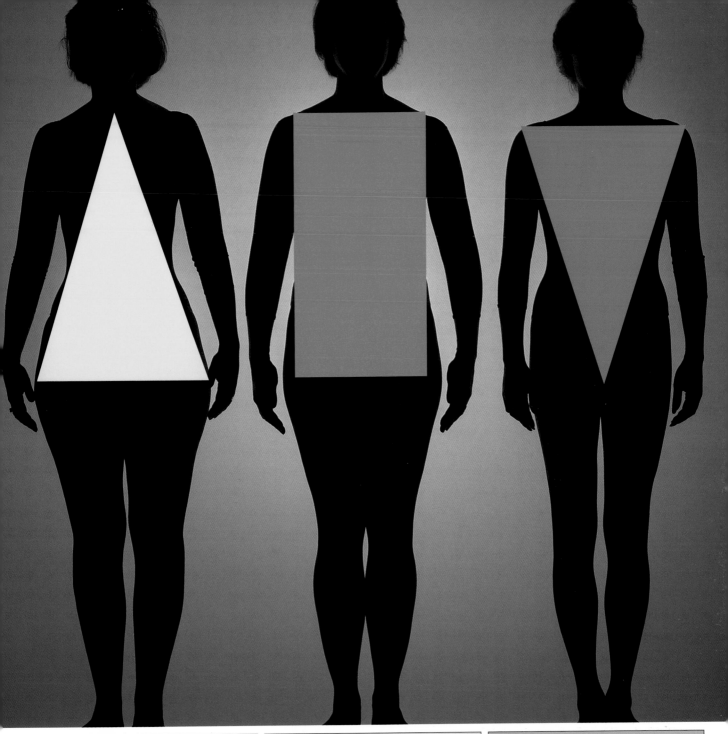

Hips Wider Than Shoulders

Figure looks smaller above waist than below. Narrow and sloping shoulders often put figure in this category. On full-figured women, fullness is through seat, hips, and thighs. Flattering pattern styles fill out shoulders and bodice for more balanced appearance. Patterns with full sleeves, extended shoulders, blouson bodices, bateau necklines, and high shoulder yokes are especially appropriate. Shoulder pads broaden natural shoulders for more pleasing proportions.

Shoulders, Waist & Hips Equally Wide

Waist is not clearly indented because it is large in proportion to hips. On full-figured women, fullness is carried in middle of body through waistline and abdomen. On slender women, figure looks fairly straight up and down. Flattering pattern styles bypass natural waistline; examples include chemise and princess-seamed dresses, overblouses and tunics, loosely fitted jackets, and layered separates.

Shoulders Wider Than Hips

Figure looks larger above waist than below. On full-figured women, fullness is carried through bustline and midriff. On slender women, broad shoulders or developed upper body muscles resulting from athletic pursuit may put figure in this category. Flattering pattern styles fill out hips for more balanced appearance. Recommended fashions are full skirts, dresses with shirring or draping across hips, and pants or skirts with soft pleats.

Shoulder Contours

Use your life-sized figure outline to analyze shoulder slope. If your shoulders have average slope, pattern shoulder seams will slant the right amount for good fit; however, your shoulders can have average slope but vary from pattern standards for shoulder length. You will need to make a pattern adjustment to increase or decrease shoulder seam length.

If your shoulders slope more or less than average, or one shoulder slopes more than the other, correct the pattern fit before you cut. When the shoulder seams are adjusted, the entire garment looks better. Sloping shoulders and narrow shoulders are often found together; so are square and broad shoulders. Combine fitting adjustments for pattern seam length and slope if you have more than one problem area.

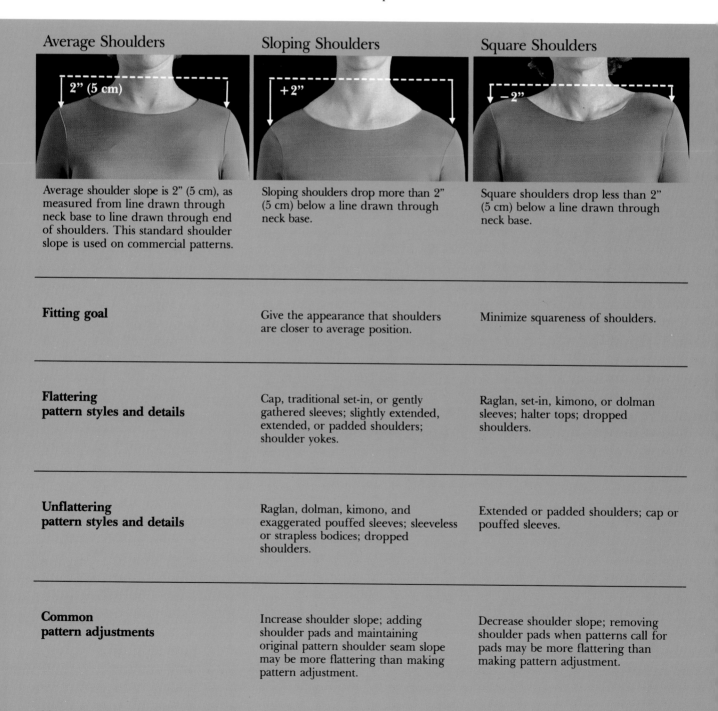

	Average Shoulders	Sloping Shoulders	Square Shoulders
	Average shoulder slope is 2" (5 cm), as measured from line drawn through neck base to line drawn through end of shoulders. This standard shoulder slope is used on commercial patterns.	Sloping shoulders drop more than 2" (5 cm) below a line drawn through neck base.	Square shoulders drop less than 2" (5 cm) below a line drawn through neck base.
Fitting goal		Give the appearance that shoulders are closer to average position.	Minimize squareness of shoulders.
Flattering pattern styles and details		Cap, traditional set-in, or gently gathered sleeves; slightly extended, extended, or padded shoulders; shoulder yokes.	Raglan, set-in, kimono, or dolman sleeves; halter tops; dropped shoulders.
Unflattering pattern styles and details		Raglan, dolman, kimono, and exaggerated pouffed sleeves; sleeveless or strapless bodices; dropped shoulders.	Extended or padded shoulders; cap or pouffed sleeves.
Common pattern adjustments		Increase shoulder slope; adding shoulder pads and maintaining original pattern shoulder seam slope may be more flattering than making pattern adjustment.	Decrease shoulder slope; removing shoulder pads when patterns call for pads may be more flattering than making pattern adjustment.

Arm Contours

Study the arm shape on your life-sized figure outline to see if your arms are average, full, or thin. You can avoid most sleeve fitting problems by choosing relaxed or dramatic sleeve styles, which do not fit closely. Traditional sleeves, fitted closely with darts or an eased area at the elbow, are most likely to require fitting adjustments. Even if you need no pattern adjustments for arm contours, sleeve length adjustments may be required. All patterns provide printed adjustment lines for this simple fitting step.

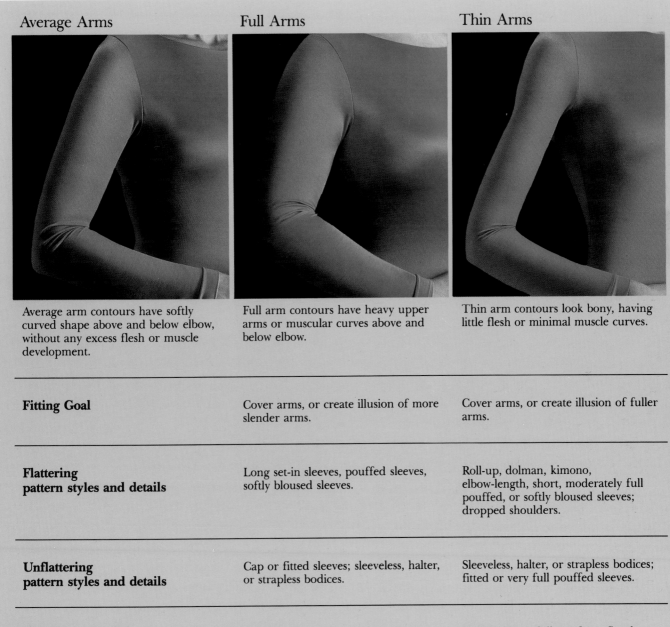

Average Arms	Full Arms	Thin Arms
Average arm contours have softly curved shape above and below elbow, without any excess flesh or muscle development.	Full arm contours have heavy upper arms or muscular curves above and below elbow.	Thin arm contours look bony, having little flesh or minimal muscle curves.
Fitting Goal	Cover arms, or create illusion of more slender arms.	Cover arms, or create illusion of fuller arms.
Flattering pattern styles and details	Long set-in sleeves, pouffed sleeves, softly bloused sleeves.	Roll-up, dolman, kimono, elbow-length, short, moderately full pouffed, or softly bloused sleeves; dropped shoulders.
Unflattering pattern styles and details	Cap or fitted sleeves; sleeveless, halter, or strapless bodices.	Sleeveless, halter, or strapless bodices; fitted or very full pouffed sleeves.
Common pattern adjustments	Add to upper arm on fitted sleeves and set-in sleeves.	Remove some fullness from fitted sleeves and set-in sleeves.

Waist Contours

Use a combination of measurements and a visual assessment of figure contours to judge whether or not your waist is average in proportion to hips. For pattern sizing, the average waist is 9½" to 10" (24 to 25.5 cm) smaller than hips. On a life-sized figure outline, there is an obvious waist indentation. A more pronounced indentation and a shorter waist measurement indicate a small waist. Little waist definition and a longer waist measurement indicate a thick waist.

If your waist varies from pattern standards, pay special attention to selecting flattering styles. At first, a small waist can seem like an asset worth accenting; however, if you have a full bust, full hips, or are short-waisted, a small waist can make these features look more exaggerated. Often the best strategy for a small or thick waist is camouflage. Styles such as overblouses, tunics, and chemise dresses that have neither waist seams nor waist shaping are often excellent choices.

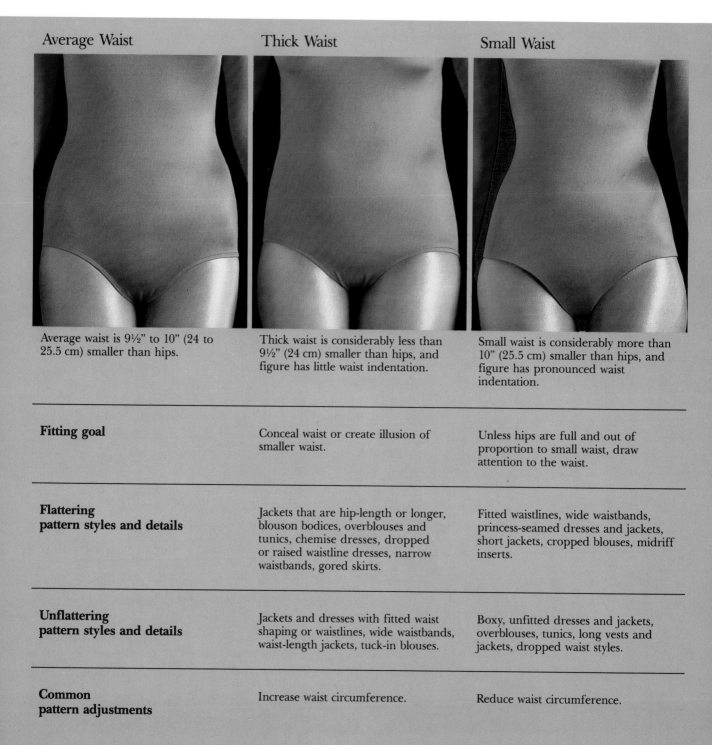

Average Waist	Thick Waist	Small Waist
Average waist is 9½" to 10" (24 to 25.5 cm) smaller than hips.	Thick waist is considerably less than 9½" (24 cm) smaller than hips, and figure has little waist indentation.	Small waist is considerably more than 10" (25.5 cm) smaller than hips, and figure has pronounced waist indentation.
Fitting goal	Conceal waist or create illusion of smaller waist.	Unless hips are full and out of proportion to small waist, draw attention to the waist.
Flattering pattern styles and details	Jackets that are hip-length or longer, blouson bodices, overblouses and tunics, chemise dresses, dropped or raised waistline dresses, narrow waistbands, gored skirts.	Fitted waistlines, wide waistbands, princess-seamed dresses and jackets, short jackets, cropped blouses, midriff inserts.
Unflattering pattern styles and details	Jackets and dresses with fitted waist shaping or waistlines, wide waistbands, waist-length jackets, tuck-in blouses.	Boxy, unfitted dresses and jackets, overblouses, tunics, long vests and jackets, dropped waist styles.
Common pattern adjustments	Increase waist circumference.	Reduce waist circumference.

Hip Contours

The clearest way to analyze hips is to compare waist and hip measurements. Standard pattern sizing defines average hips as 9½" to 10" (24 to 25.5 cm) larger than the waist. Fuller or slimmer hips need pattern adjustments for good fit and careful style selection for a flattering image.

Misses' patterns are sized for a hipline 9" (23 cm) below the waist. Petite figures may have a higher hipline. On full figures the hipline may be lower than 9" (23 cm). A basic adjustment to position the hipline properly can make a big improvement in garment fit and eliminate the need for more extensive adjustments.

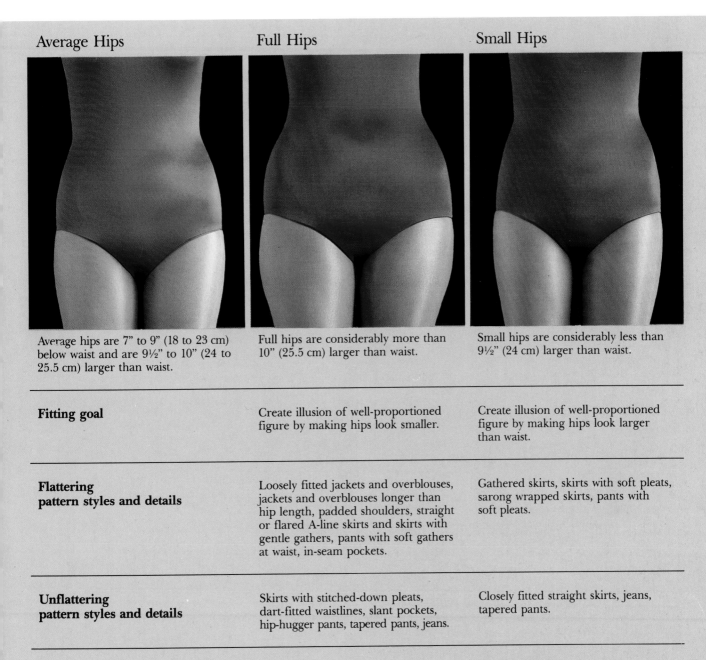

	Average Hips	Full Hips	Small Hips
	Average hips are 7" to 9" (18 to 23 cm) below waist and are 9½" to 10" (24 to 25.5 cm) larger than waist.	Full hips are considerably more than 10" (25.5 cm) larger than waist.	Small hips are considerably less than 9½" (24 cm) larger than waist.
Fitting goal		Create illusion of well-proportioned figure by making hips look smaller.	Create illusion of well-proportioned figure by making hips look larger than waist.
Flattering pattern styles and details		Loosely fitted jackets and overblouses, jackets and overblouses longer than hip length, padded shoulders, straight or flared A-line skirts and skirts with gentle gathers, pants with soft gathers at waist, in-seam pockets.	Gathered skirts, skirts with soft pleats, sarong wrapped skirts, pants with soft pleats.
Unflattering pattern styles and details		Skirts with stitched-down pleats, dart-fitted waistlines, slant pockets, hip-hugger pants, tapered pants, jeans.	Closely fitted straight skirts, jeans, tapered pants.
Common pattern adjustments		Increase hip circumference, make waist darts deeper, or convert darts to soft gathers.	Reduce hip circumference, make waist darts shallower.

Thigh Contours

Thigh contours affect the way pants and skirts fit. Compare thigh contours as shown on your life-sized figure outline with average thigh contours. If your thighs are fuller or thinner than the average, pants with traditional, close fit pose the most fitting problems. Patterns with a more relaxed fit will help you avoid making pattern adjustments or will require only minor fitting changes.

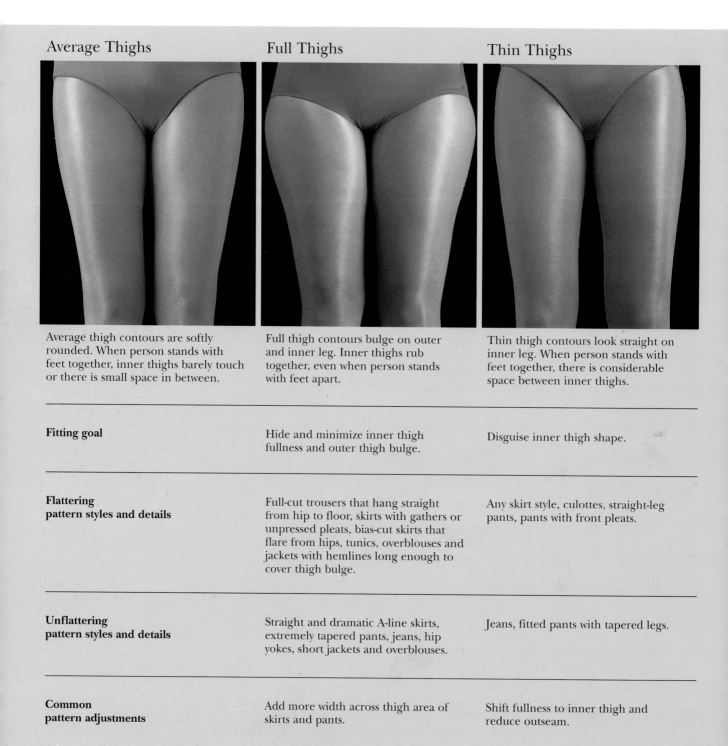

	Average Thighs	Full Thighs	Thin Thighs
	Average thigh contours are softly rounded. When person stands with feet together, inner thighs barely touch or there is small space in between.	Full thigh contours bulge on outer and inner leg. Inner thighs rub together, even when person stands with feet apart.	Thin thigh contours look straight on inner leg. When person stands with feet together, there is considerable space between inner thighs.
Fitting goal		Hide and minimize inner thigh fullness and outer thigh bulge.	Disguise inner thigh shape.
Flattering pattern styles and details		Full-cut trousers that hang straight from hip to floor, skirts with gathers or unpressed pleats, bias-cut skirts that flare from hips, tunics, overblouses and jackets with hemlines long enough to cover thigh bulge.	Any skirt style, culottes, straight-leg pants, pants with front pleats.
Unflattering pattern styles and details		Straight and dramatic A-line skirts, extremely tapered pants, jeans, hip yokes, short jackets and overblouses.	Jeans, fitted pants with tapered legs.
Common pattern adjustments		Add more width across thigh area of skirts and pants.	Shift fullness to inner thigh and reduce outseam.

Bust Profile

Your body profile helps you compare your figure with average pattern contours at bust, abdomen, and seat. As when analyzing your figure from the front, avoid relying on judgments based on your reflection in a mirror. Instead, have someone take instant photographs of you from the side. Use them to help you make an honest, objective analysis.

A well-fitted bra can improve bust contours, especially as viewed in profile. Minimizer bras control full bustlines, underwire bras provide firm support, padded bras increase bust contours, and soft knit bras conform to the natural bust shape. Some brands provide informative package labels to guide you toward making figure-flattering purchases. If you have experienced bust fitting problems in the past, or your figure analysis leaves you unsatisfied with what you have found, changing to a different type or size of bra may be a quick way to solve a fitting problem.

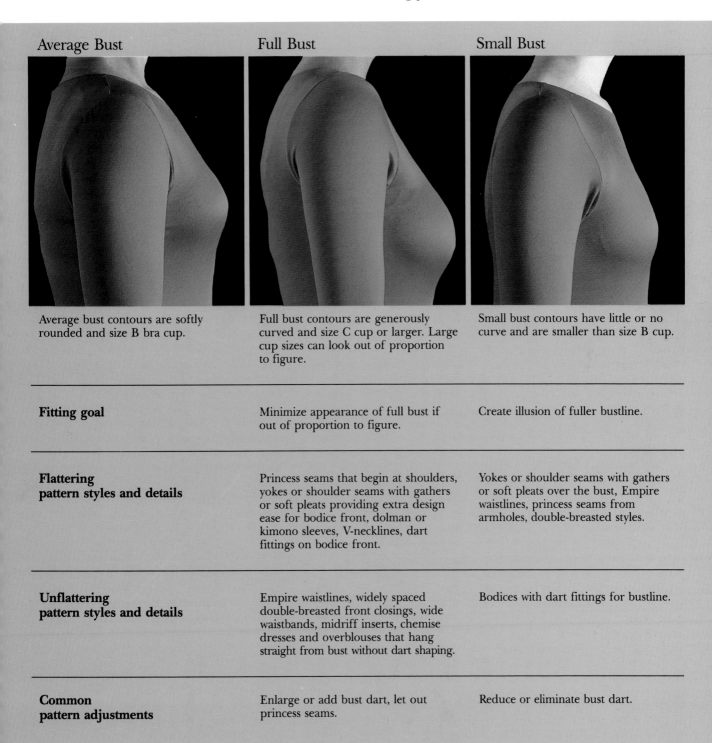

	Average Bust	Full Bust	Small Bust
	Average bust contours are softly rounded and size B bra cup.	Full bust contours are generously curved and size C cup or larger. Large cup sizes can look out of proportion to figure.	Small bust contours have little or no curve and are smaller than size B cup.
Fitting goal		Minimize appearance of full bust if out of proportion to figure.	Create illusion of fuller bustline.
Flattering pattern styles and details		Princess seams that begin at shoulders, yokes or shoulder seams with gathers or soft pleats providing extra design ease for bodice front, dolman or kimono sleeves, V-necklines, dart fittings on bodice front.	Yokes or shoulder seams with gathers or soft pleats over the bust, Empire waistlines, princess seams from armholes, double-breasted styles.
Unflattering pattern styles and details		Empire waistlines, widely spaced double-breasted front closings, wide waistbands, midriff inserts, chemise dresses and overblouses that hang straight from bust without dart shaping.	Bodices with dart fittings for bustline.
Common pattern adjustments		Enlarge or add bust dart, let out princess seams.	Reduce or eliminate bust dart.

Abdomen Profile

Abdominal contours can change from time to time because they are affected by weight loss or gain, exercise, childbearing, and other influences. The abdominal curve is also affected by posture. If you are swaybacked, you may also have an abdomen that is more rounded than the average.

Average Abdomen	Full Abdomen	Flat Abdomen
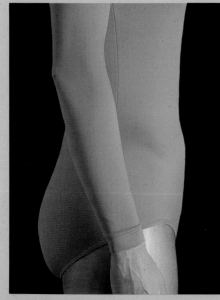	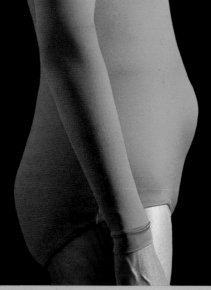	
Average abdominal contours are slightly rounded below natural waist.	Full abdominal contours are more rounded than average and curve prominently.	Flat abdominal contours look straight below waist or look hollow. Hipbones may protrude.
Fitting goal	Minimize or camouflage abdominal shape.	Create illusion of slight fullness in front and camouflage hipbones.
Flattering pattern styles and details	Pants and skirts with unpressed pleats or tucks, pants and skirts with soft gathers set to sides of abdominal curve, elasticized waistlines, narrow waistbands, gored skirts, bias-cut skirts, chemise dresses, blouson bodices to hips, overblouses, jackets long enough to cover abdomen.	Pants and skirts with gathers or unpressed pleats, blouson bodices, overblouses with low waistlines, tunics, dropped waistlines, chemise dresses, peplums.
Unflattering pattern styles and details	Pants and skirts dart-fitted to waistbands, contoured waistbands, wide waistbands, double-breasted jackets, fly-front zipper closings.	Pants and skirts that fit closely, including those dart-fitted to waistband.
Common pattern adjustments	Add length at center front waistline for skirts and pants; for full lower abdomen, add length to front crotch extension for pants.	Convert front darts to gathers at waistline, decrease front crotch length on pants, take in side seams on front of skirts and pants.

Seat Profile

Like abdominal contours, seat contours are affected by maturity, diet, and muscle tone. The older you are, the less likely you are to have average seat contours; the muscles in the seat tend to create flatter contours as you age. A swaybacked posture is a distinctive seat contour that requires careful pattern selection and fitting adjustments.

Seat contours are critical for fitting pants. It is important that the crotch seam curve match your figure shape. If you have successfully fitted the crotch seam, your seat contours will look more attractive no matter how they compare with the average contour.

	Average Seat	Full Seat	Flat Seat	Swaybacked Seat
	Average seat contours have small, high curve.	Full seat contours have generous, rounded curve.	Flat seat contours have little or no curve.	Swaybacked seat contours seem to jut out from hollow just below natural waist. Waist may be small in proportion to hips.
Fitting goal		Minimize or conceal fullness of curve.	Create illusion of shape.	Minimize hollow below waist, and create illusion of smaller hips.
Flattering pattern styles and details		Pants and skirts with relaxed fit or with unpressed pleats, gored or slightly flared skirts, straight-cut pants, waistline gathers, slightly oversized tops, chemise dresses, jackets long enough to cover seat.	Jumpsuits with waistline seam, pants and skirts with pleats or gathers in back or with gathers from hip yoke, dirndl or gored skirts, culottes, harem pants, waistbands with elasticized backs, elasticized waistlines with sewn-on waistband, blouson tops with dropped waistlines.	Two-piece dresses, dresses and jumpsuits with waistline seam, pants and skirts with unpressed pleats or gathers, gored skirts with four or six panels, waistbands with elasticized backs, elasticized waistbands with sewn-on waistband, boxy jackets long enough to cover back waist area.
Unflattering pattern styles and details		Close fit above or below waist, tapered pants, dropped waistlines, hip yokes, short jackets, back interest.	Bias-cut skirts, closely fitted pants and skirts.	Hip yokes, waist-length jackets, center back zippers, skirts with stitched-down pleats or pressed pleats, any style that is formfitting in upper back hip area.
Common pattern adjustments		Increase depth of back waistline darts, lengthen back crotch seam on pants.	Eliminate back waistline darts or convert them to gathers, shorten back crotch seam on pants.	Shorten center back seam at waistline on pants and skirts.

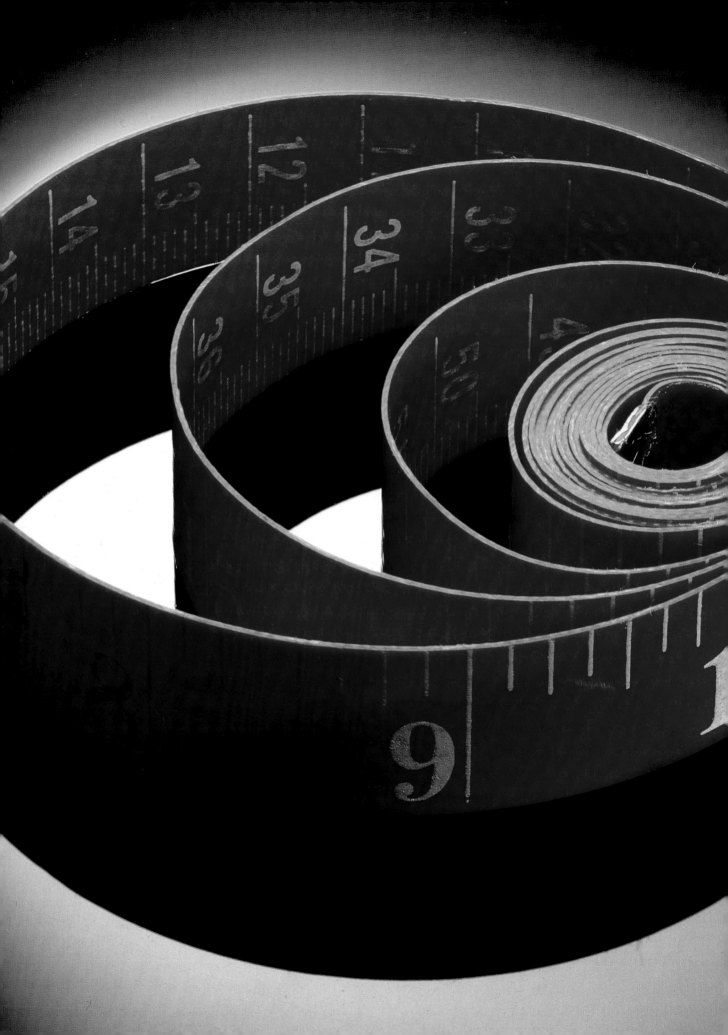

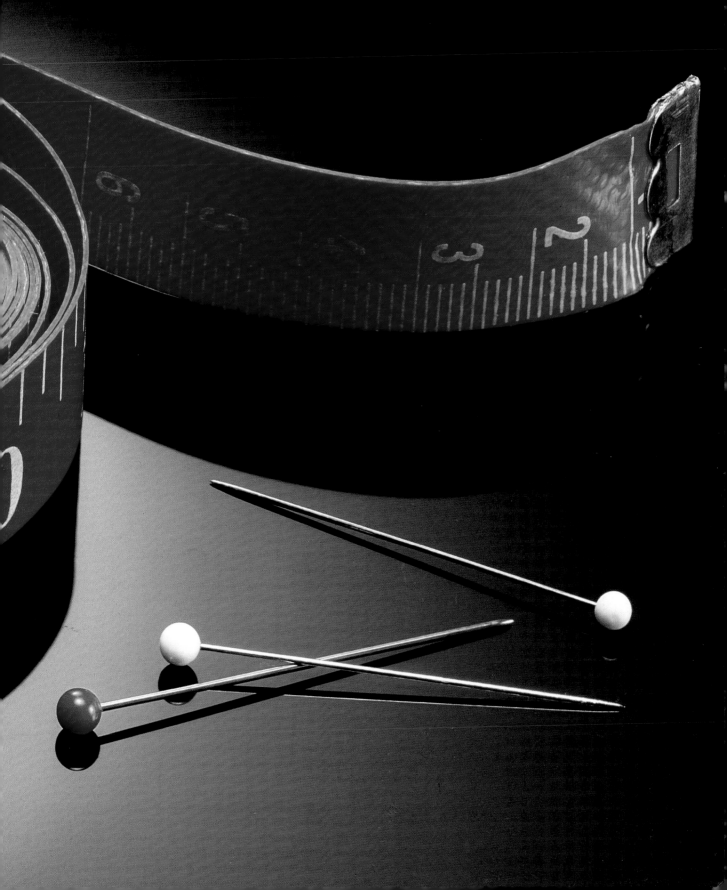

Body Measurements

Taking Measurements

Four figure measurements are required for choosing a pattern size: high bust, bust, waist, and hips. Take these measurements honestly and accurately, using a nonstretch measuring tape. All measurements should be snug, but not tight. If your measuring tape is worn, it is inexpensive insurance to buy a replacement for fitting. Also, ask someone to take and record your measurements. Taking your own measurements is awkward and often inaccurate.

The clothing you wear and your posture affect the accuracy of your figure measurements. Wear comfortable, well-fitted undergarments that do not distort your natural figure contours. Avoid wearing anything that causes figure bulges or feels tight, especially at the midriff, waist, abdomen, and thighs. Do not wear a girdle or control-top pantyhose unless you will wear them with garments you sew. Wear comfortable shoes of a heel height you ordinarily prefer. Stand normally and relax, looking straight ahead. Do not hold your breath or stand stiffly.

Using your bust or high bust, waist, and hip measurements, select the pattern size that matches or comes close to these three measurements. Compare your measurements with those on the chart on page 41 to determine your pattern size. Finding a perfect match is unnecessary. Patterns are based on averages, allowing pattern companies to provide a range of sizes appropriate for the majority of their customers. Through pattern adjustments, you can customize a standard pattern size to fit your figure. The chart below helps you choose the best pattern size for the garment, by making a suitable compromise when all your figure measurements do not match the pattern size.

Pattern Type and Selection Guide

Pattern Type	Size Selection Guide
Blouse, dress, jacket, coat, vest, or jumpsuit	Choose pattern size closest to your bust (or high bust) measurement.
Pants, fitted skirt, skirt or pants with pleats or gathers at waistline and relaxed hip fit, skirt with stitched-down pleats or other traditional hip fit	Choose pattern size closest to your hip measurement unless hips are two sizes larger than waist; then select in-between size, and make smaller adjustment to waist and hips.
Skirt with exaggerated fullness at waist and hip	Choose pattern size closest to your waist measurement.
Coordinated separates	Choose pattern size closest to your bust (or high bust) measurement.

Basic Figure Measurements

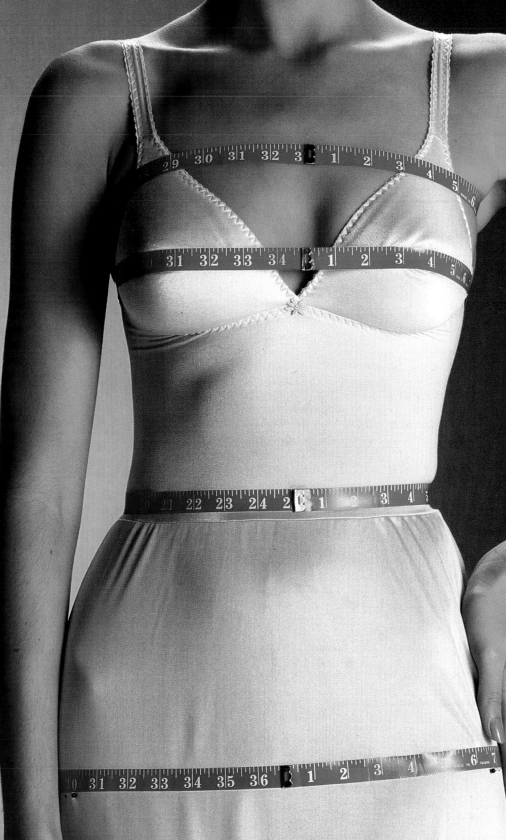

High bust. Measure around figure high under arms, across widest part of back and above full bust.

Bust. Without pulling tape too tight, measure over fullest part of bust, keeping tape straight and parallel to floor.

Waist. Tie narrow elastic or cord around waist to mark natural position. Measure waist at this point, keeping tape parallel to floor. Keep tape snug, but loose enough to slide around waistline.

Hips. Mark fullest part of hip with pin. This is usually 7" to 9" (18 to 23 cm) below natural waist, above crease at top of leg. Measure with bottom edge of tape at pin; keep tape parallel to floor.

Choosing a Pattern Size

The right pattern size simplifies fitting because it eliminates the need for extensive adjustments. To find the best pattern size, you must decide whether to use your bust or high bust measurement. Compare the two measurements. If there is a difference of 2" (5 cm) or more between them, use the high bust measurement instead of the full bust measurement to select a pattern size.

Such a difference normally indicates that you have a full bust and a cup size larger than the standard B cup used for sizing patterns. By using the smaller measurement to select a pattern size, you will select a pattern that gives a better fit through the neckline, shoulders, armholes, upper back, and sleeves. You may have to make adjustments to the bodice front to accommodate your full natural bustline.

If your figure measurements fall between two pattern sizes, in general choose the smaller size. This gives you a better fit in garment areas that are time-consuming to adjust, such as the neckline, shoulders, and armholes.

Misses' figure type is the average or standard figure used for pattern sizing. This is a well-proportioned and developed figure about 5'5" to 5'6" (1.65 to 1.68 m) tall, without shoes.

Miss Petite figure type is well-proportioned and developed like the Misses' type, but with shorter length proportions and about 5'2" to 5'4" (1.57 to 1.63 m) tall.

Half-size figure type is fully developed like the Women's figure type, but shorter, about 5'2" to 5'3" (1.57 to 1.60 m) tall. The waist is also larger in proportion to the bust, and shoulders are narrower.

Women's figure type is the same height as the Misses' type, but fuller and larger at the bust, waist, and hips.

Although some pattern catalogs contain styles sized especially for Miss Petites, Women, and Half-sizes, the selection is limited. If you have one of these figure types, you can select the Misses' pattern size that comes closest to your basic figure measurements and then adjust the pattern to fit your personal proportions. Although this means extra effort before cutting, the Misses' size gives you a wider variety of fashion styles from which to choose.

Figure Size Chart

Misses': Inches

Size	6	8	10	12	14	16	18	20	22	24
Bust	30½	31½	32½	34	36	38	40	42	44	46
Waist	23	24	25	26½	28	30	32	34	36	38
Hip	32½	33½	34½	36	38	40	42	44	46	48
Back Waist Length	15½	15¾	16	16¼	16½	16¾	17	17¼	17½	17¾

Misses': Centimeters

Size	6	8	10	12	14	16	18	20	22	24
Bust	78	80	83	87	92	97	102	107	112	117
Waist	58	61	64	67	71	76	81	87	92	97
Hip	83	85	88	92	97	102	107	112	117	122
Back Waist Length	39.5	40	40.5	41.5	42	42.5	43	44	44.5	45

Miss Petite: Inches

Size	6mp	8mp	10mp	12mp	14mp	16mp
Bust	30½	31½	32½	34	36	38
Waist	23½	24½	25½	27	28½	30½
Hip	32½	33½	34½	36	38	40
Back Waist Length	14½	14¾	15	15¼	15½	15¾

Miss Petite: Centimeters

Size	6mp	8mp	10mp	12mp	14mp	16mp
Bust	78	80	83	87	92	97
Waist	60	62	65	69	73	78
Hip	83	85	88	92	97	102
Back Waist Length	37	37.5	38	39	39.5	40

Half-size: Inches

Size	10½	12½	14½	16½	18½	20½	22½	24½
Bust	33	35	37	39	41	43	45	47
Waist	27	29	31	33	35	37½	40	42½
Hip	35	37	39	41	43	45½	48	50½
Back Waist Length	15	15¼	15½	15¾	15⅞	16	16⅛	16¼

Half-size: Centimeters

Size	10½	12½	14½	16½	18½	20½	22½	24½
Bust	84	89	94	99	104	109	114	119
Waist	69	74	79	84	89	96	102	108
Hip	89	94	99	104	109	116	122	128
Back Waist Length	38	39	39.5	40	40.5	40.5	41	41.5

Women's: Inches

Size	38	40	42	44	46	48	50	52
Bust	42	44	46	48	50	52	54	56
Waist	35	37	39	41½	44	46½	49	51½
Hip	44	46	48	50	52	54	56	58
Back Waist Length	17¼	17⅜	17½	17⅝	17¾	17⅞	18	18⅛

Women's: Centimeters

Size	38	40	42	44	46	48	50	52
Bust	107	112	117	122	127	132	137	142
Waist	89	94	99	105	112	118	124	131
Hip	112	117	122	127	132	137	142	147
Back Waist Length	44	44	44.5	45	45	45.5	46	46

Special Fitting Patterns

Certain patterns are designed especially to make fitting easier. Some of these patterns solve a specific fitting problem; others solve several problems. How helpful you find a special fitting pattern depends largely on which fitting adjustments you require. The *basic fitting shell* patterns represent the master patterns used by a pattern company. They are available for dresses and pants. *Multiple-sized* patterns have cutting lines for two or more pattern sizes on each pattern piece. *Preprinted adjustable* patterns solve specific fitting problems, such as shortening a pattern to Miss Petite proportions. *Fashion fitting* patterns show how to fit as you sew, usually with extra-wide seam allowances.

Basic Fitting Shells

Fitting a basic shell requires time and effort, so it is most worthwhile for difficult fitting problems. Fit the shell garment to your figure. Use it as a guide for adjusting fashion patterns. Lay fashion pattern piece on top of corresponding section from basic shell that has been adjusted for your figure. Compare to determine need for fashion pattern adjustments, remembering that shell has minimum ease allowances only. Fashion pattern may have more than minimum ease for design purposes.

Multiple-sized Patterns

Follow cutting lines for pattern size as needed if bust is one size and waist or hips are another. Blend as you cut by tapering gradually from one size into another. Do not jump more than single size at once or garment seam will look distorted. Multiple-sized patterns have three separate cutting lines but do not provide printed stitching lines for each size.

Preprinted Adjustable Patterns

Follow instructions on pattern to make adjustment as printed on pattern pieces. Some adjustable patterns furnish separate cutting lines for different figure contours, such as full bust and narrow or broad shoulders, or separate pattern pieces for flat, average, and full seats. If there is a pattern that focuses on your fitting problem, it can save you a considerable amount of time and effort. This kind of adjustment is standardized, however, so you may still have to increase or decrease it to fit your figure.

Fashion Fitting Patterns

These patterns have extra-wide seam allowances at key fitting areas. This provides sufficient room to take in or let out seams as needed. Because garment seams can be altered only limited amounts without distortion, these patterns are most successful for minor fitting changes. As a reminder that pattern has seam allowances wider than standard ⅝" (1.5 cm), use snips to mark seamline on cutout garment sections.

Pattern Adjustments

General Guidelines for Pattern Adjustments

Pattern adjustments change the measurement and shape of standard pattern pieces to fit your figure. To streamline the entire fitting process, make as many fitting changes as you can before you cut. Step-by-step instructions for specific adjustments are given on the following pages. The basic guidelines below apply to most changes you are likely to make.

Press pattern pieces with a warm, dry iron before you start. It is not accurate to work with wrinkled tissue pieces.

Pin-fit the pattern to preview how well the fashion style fits your figure. Adjust the pattern on your body, or decide how extensively you need pattern adjustments. If you need many adjustments, reconsider your choice of pattern style. Another style may fit your figure with fewer adjustments. Also, pin-fit after making pattern adjustments as a fast check of their accuracy.

Work in a logical order, completing lengthening or shortening pattern adjustments first. Then work from the top of the pattern down to make additional adjustments to fit body width and contours.

Watch for chain reactions. Adjustments on one pattern piece usually require matching adjustments on adjoining pattern sections. If you change the neckline seam, for example, you must change the neck facing to match. Sometimes a compensating rather than a matching adjustment is necessary. For example, if you lower the shoulder seams to fit sloping shoulders, you must also lower the underarm seam to retain the armhole size.

Maintain the original grainline as printed on the pattern pieces, so the finished garment hangs properly. Extend the grainline from one edge of the pattern piece to the other before cutting. This helps preserve grainline as you make adjustments.

Blend the adjusted stitching and cutting lines back into the original lines. When adjustments are blended correctly, the original shape of the pattern piece will not be distorted.

To blend a seam, draw a continuous line where one has become broken during pattern adjustment. To blend a straight line, use a ruler or straight edge, connecting the beginning and end of the new line. To blend a curved line, use a curved ruler to reconstruct the original curve of the pattern,

blending to each end from a point halfway between the broken seamline.

Blend the seamline first, then the cutting line. On multiple-sized patterns where no seamlines are marked, blend the cutting line only, and stitch the specified seam allowance, usually ⅝" (1.5 cm).

When there is a dart in the seamline, fold the dart out before blending the line. Be sure to mark all notches and darts on the new blended seamline.

Choosing an Adjustment Method

Wherever possible, two methods are given for the most common pattern adjustments: the minor, or in-seam, method and the major, or cut-and-slide, method. Choose one method or the other, depending on how much of an adjustment you need to make.

Minor in-seam pattern adjustments are quick and easy, because you can mark them directly on the printed pattern within the seam allowance or on the pattern tissue margin. In-seam methods have narrow limitations. Usually you can add or subtract no more than ⅜" to ½" (1 to 1.3 cm).

In the photos, to clarify where an addition would normally be marked on the margin of the tissue pattern, the margin has been trimmed and a contrasting tissue placed under the pattern. This procedure is not necessary on patterns that have not been used previously, because they have generous tissue margins around them.

Major cut-and-slide pattern adjustments allow you to add or subtract greater amounts than in-seam methods and to make adjustments exactly where they are needed to fit your figure. Cut-and-slide methods also have limits, usually to a maximum of 2" (5 cm). The specific amount is stated with the step-by-step instructions. Do not attempt to adjust beyond the stated maximums or you will distort the shape of the pattern pieces and cause the finished garment to hang off-grain. It will also be more difficult to make matching or compensating adjustments on adjoining pattern sections.

If you need a greater adjustment than cut-and-slide methods allow, consider working with another pattern size. Or distribute the adjustment over additional pattern seams and details instead of concentrating the adjustment in one area.

How to Pin-fit Patterns

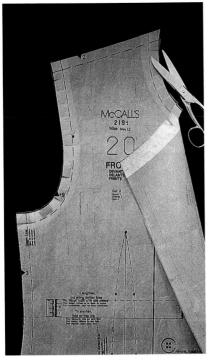

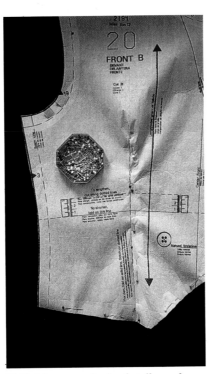

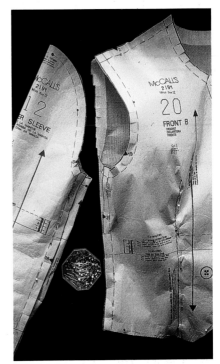

1) Reinforce neckline and armhole edges of major pattern pieces with lightweight fusible interfacing. Clip curves to seamline. Omit minor pieces, such as collars and facings.

2) Fold out and pin details such as darts, pleats, or tucks on major pattern pieces. Fold up hems, and pin in place.

3) Lap and pin front and back pattern pieces on shoulder and side, with seamlines matching. Pin or baste sleeve into armhole.

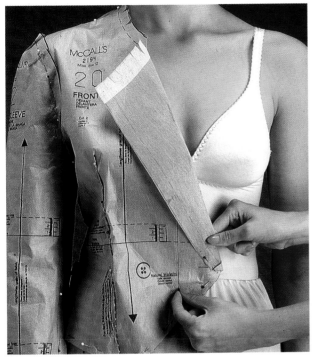

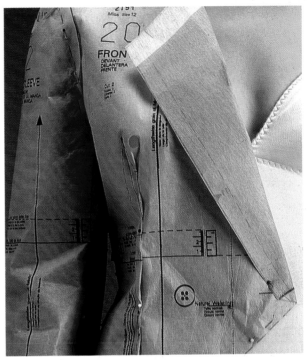

4) Try on pinned pattern. Pin center front and back to a close-fitting undergarment.

5) Mark bust point. Determine adjustments needed, and mark on the pattern while tissue pattern is on body. Remove excess length by pinning tucks in pattern pieces. Increase pattern size by adjusting seam allowances or repinning darts.

Basic Length Adjustments

Before making any other pattern adjustments, adjust the length of pattern pieces to fit your personal length proportions. If your figure is close to average, basic length adjustments may be the only changes needed on most patterns.

Basic length adjustments are made in two areas: above and below the waist. Use your back waist length figure measurement to determine the correct pattern length *above* the waist. To determine the correct pattern length *below* the waist, measure from the waist in back to the proposed hemline. Make these length adjustments using the adjustment lines on the pattern pieces.

Adjustments for Special Figures

Most people can make basic length adjustments by using the printed lengthening and shortening lines; however, if you have a rounded back, adjust the pattern length above the waist, as on page 86. If you have a full bust, adjust the pattern length above the waist, as on page 74.

For Half-size or Miss Petite figure types, reduce the pattern length proportionately, by dividing the total adjustment into four smaller amounts. Shorten the pattern at the chest and the sleeve cap and at the hipline, in addition to using the printed adjustment lines above and below the waist.

Standard pattern shortening adjustments for Miss Petite remove ¼" (6 mm) at chest, ¾" (2 cm) above waist, 1" (2.5 cm) at hips, and 1" (2.5 cm) below waist to shorten pattern by 3" (7.5 cm). Standard adjustments for Half-sizes are similar, but the chest adjustment is omitted because armhole size does not need to be reduced. Customize standard length adjustments to suit your personal proportions.

How to Determine Length Adjustments

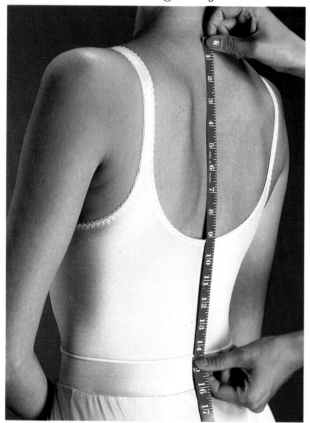

Above the waist. Measure back waist length from prominent bone at back of neck to natural waistline. Compare with back waist length measurement for your pattern size given on pattern envelope to determine how much to adjust bodice front and back patterns.

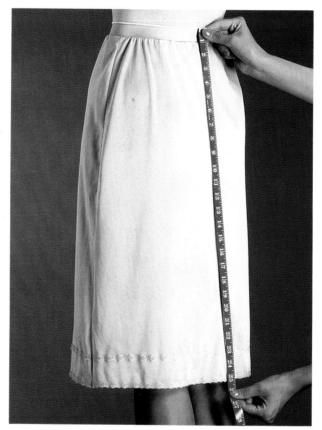

Below the waist. Measure at center back from waist to proposed garment hemline, or use a garment of correct length to determine this measurement. Compare with finished garment length given on back of pattern envelope to determine how much to adjust skirt front and back patterns.

How to Shorten Patterns

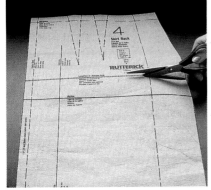

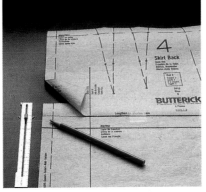

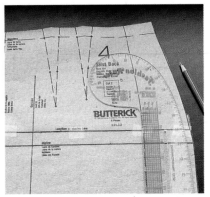

1) Cut pattern on the printed adjustment lines. If skirt pattern provides no adjustment lines, cut off excess length at bottom edge.

2) Lap cut sections. Overlap equals total amount pattern must be shortened. Tape sections together, keeping grainline straight.

3) Blend stitching and cutting lines. Make matching adjustments on back and front pattern pieces.

How to Lengthen Patterns

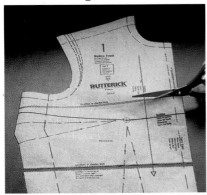

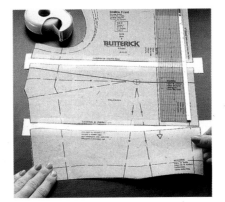

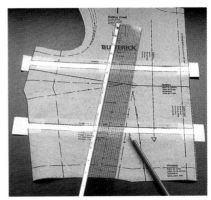

1) Cut pattern on the printed adjustment lines. If skirt pattern provides no adjustment lines, add length at bottom edge.

2) Spread cut sections the amount needed. Place paper underneath to bridge gap. Tape sections in place, keeping grainline straight.

3) Blend stitching and cutting lines. Make matching adjustments on back and front patterns.

How to Shorten Patterns for Half-sizes and Petites

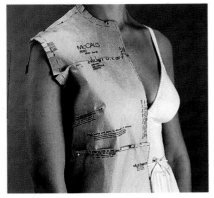

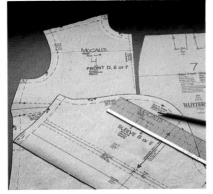

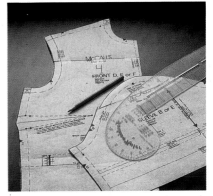

1) Pin-fit or measure pattern to determine how much length to remove across chest above armhole notches, at adjustment line above waist, at hipline, and at adjustment line below waist.

2) Draw adjustment lines on front and back, midway between armhole and shoulder seam notches. Draw similar line across sleeve cap. Draw hip adjustment line 7" (18 cm) below waist on skirt front and back.

3) Cut pattern pieces on each adjustment line; lap to shorten. Shorten back and front patterns equally. Shorten sleeve cap by same amount removed from bodice at chest.

Fitting with Darts

Darts shape flat fabric to fit curves at bust, waist, seat, and hips. On closely fitted pattern styles, there may also be elbow darts to fit the sleeves, and shoulder seam or neckline darts to fit the upper back. Darts come in and out of fashion, but they are generally found on patterns featuring traditional fit.

Darts are a valuable fitting help because the depth, length, shape, and location can be changed to improve garment fit. Darts shape the garment for an average figure, but if your contours curve more than average, *take in* darts for a better fit. If your contours are flatter than average, *let out* darts so they are less deep. Do not take in darts to remove excess fabric from garments that are too loose, or let out

darts to add more room when garments are too tight. An adjustment in the dart will change the length of the seam, so you will need to adjust the seam to compensate for the change.

To improve fit, you may want to add darts to patterns that do not have them. Full-busted figures often benefit from the addition of bust darts to the front bodice of dresses and blouses, for example. In a textured fabric or an allover print, the added dart will be barely noticeable. If warranted by your fabric, figure shape, or pattern style, you can also convert darts to less-fitted details, such as soft pleats or gentle gathers, for a more flattering appearance.

Adjusting Darts on Patterns

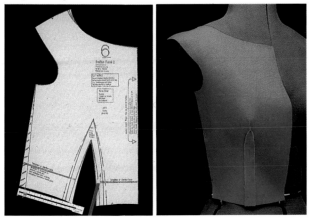

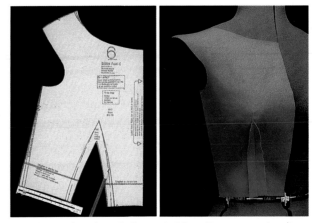

Mark *within* printed dart stitching lines to make dart *shallower* if figure contours are flatter than average. Shallow dart takes up less fabric for a less-contoured shape. Make a compensating adjustment at side seam.

Mark *outside* printed dart stitching lines to make dart *deeper* if your figure contours are fuller and more rounded than average. Deep dart takes up more fabric for more shaping. Make a compensating adjustment at side seam.

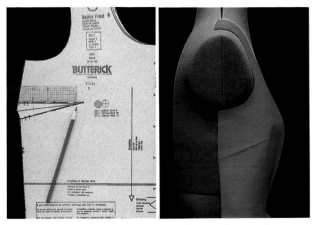

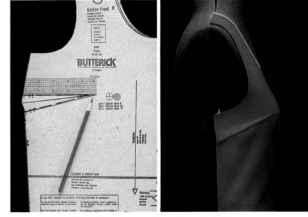

Shorten darts by marking new dart point on dart foldline. Blend stitching lines. Darts should end at least 1" (2.5 cm) short of bust point. Darts should stop at least ½" (1.3 cm) short of fullest part of hips.

Lengthen darts by extending dart foldline past original dart point to mark new point; then draw new stitching lines.

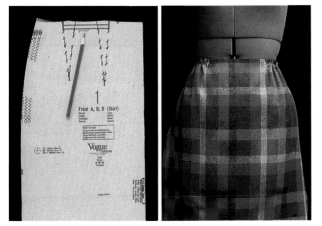

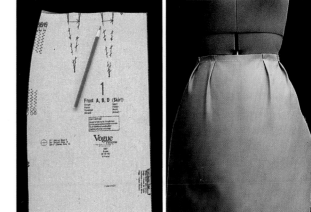

Convert darts to gathers when figure contours are flatter than average, or when using a print, plaid, or stripe that looks distorted with darts.

Convert darts to unpressed tucks or pleats for a soft look. Gathers and pleats are typical dart substitutes on relaxed or dramatic pattern styles.

Fitting As You Sew

To allow for maximum adjustments as you sew, cut out the garment with extra-wide seam allowances wherever you know or suspect you might need additional length or width. Pin or machine-baste on original seamline; then try on the garment and make any fitting changes you need.

Cut wide seams only if working with an appropriate fabric. Fabrics such as velvets and vinyls are not suitable because they can be marred by pins and removed stitches. Stripes and plaids that require matching may also be unsuitable for this technique.

Where to Add Wider Seam Allowances for Fitting

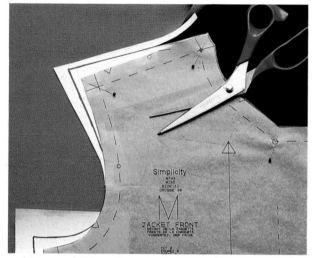

Shoulder and armhole seams. Cut 1" (2.5 cm) seam allowance at shoulder edge to allow for square shoulder adjustment; taper to normal ⅝" (1.5 cm) seam allowance at neckline. Cut extra-wide seam allowances at armhole edge and underarm to allow for square and forward thrust shoulders.

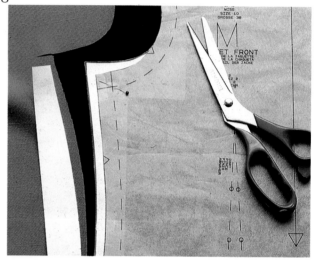

Side seams. Cut 1" (2.5 cm) seam allowances to provide as much as 1½" (3.8 cm) additional circumference for fitting bust, waist, and hips.

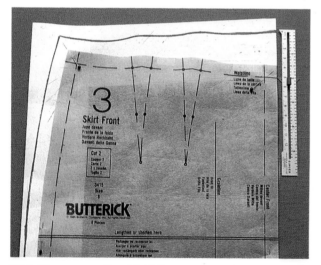

Waistline seam. Cut 1" (2.5 cm) seam allowances on front and back bodice to allow up to ¾" (2 cm) more length if needed. Wide seam allowances can also be used to fit garment when one hip is higher than other. On pants and skirts, taper cutting line 2" (5 cm) higher at center front to provide extra seam allowance for fitting full abdomen.

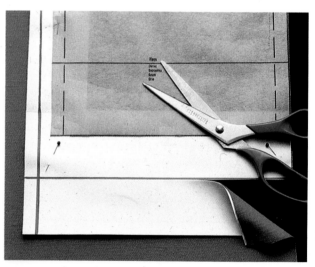

Hemline. Cut extra length at lower edge to allow for hemline changes. Hemline can be affected by change in heel height of shoes, undergarments, and accessories such as belts.

How to Fit As You Sew

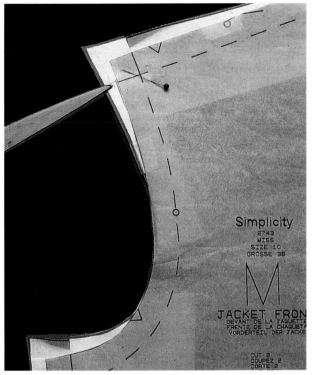

1) Mark original garment stitching lines after cutting out pattern with extra-wide seam allowances. Be sure that marking lines are removable. Baste on marked stitching lines. Or pin seams together, placing pins with points down.

2) Try on garment after major seams have been basted or pinned. Adjust to fit, using extra-wide seam allowances if you need more room.

3) Mark new stitching lines where garment requires change; mark along pins on wrong side of garment.

4) Stitch as marked. Trim seams and finish seam allowances. Wide seam allowances on curved seams cause pulling and puckering.

Fitting Shoulders

It is essential that the shoulder seams on a pattern fit the width and the slope of your shoulders. Garments that hang from the shoulders, such as blouses, dresses, and jackets, must fit well through the shoulder area or the entire garment will drape off-grain. Because the shoulder seams influence how the garment fits through the bodice, armholes, and sleeves, improving the shoulder fit may solve problems in other areas as well. When fitted correctly, the shoulder seams of a garment should fall on top of your natural shoulders. The seams should also look straight when viewed in profile, without being pulled toward the back or toward the front.

The basic concept of fitting is to start at the top and work down, so shoulder seams should be adjusted after making any basic lengthening and shortening adjustments. Most of the shoulder seam adjustments involve minor changes for slope and width. Another common adjustment repositions the shoulder seams for forward thrust, a stance in which the outer edge of the shoulders and arms is set closer to the front of the body than the average.

Depending upon your shoulder contours, you may need to combine two or more adjustments. For example, a half-size figure may have narrow and sloping shoulders. Forward thrust shoulders also might belong to the sloping shoulders category. Broad shoulders can be square as well. The methods for a major adjustment given on the following pages make it easy to combine pattern adjustments.

How to Determine Pattern Adjustments

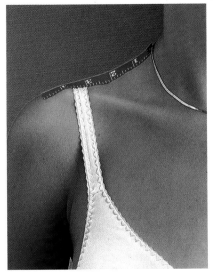

Measure your shoulder width from neck base to shoulder joint. Neck base is underneath the earlobe. Mark neck base by wearing simple necklace. To locate shoulder joint, raise arm and feel indentation at socket. To determine shoulder slope, compare with figures on page 28.

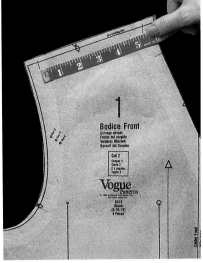

Measure length of pattern shoulder seam between stitching lines at neckline and armhole. Compare your shoulder width with pattern measurement to learn how much adjustment, if any, is needed. When the pattern has a lowered neckline, pin-fit rather than measure to determine shoulder seam length.

Pin-fit pattern to determine if adjustments for shoulder slope or forward thrust are needed and to judge shoulder width when pattern neckline is below neck base. If pattern calls for shoulder pads, wear pads while pin-fitting. Use pin-fitting also to analyze need for shoulder adjustments when pattern has dropped or extended shoulders.

Sloping Shoulders

Poor fit occurs when natural shoulders slant more than pattern shoulder seams. Wrinkles form diagonally from neckline to armhole. Use shoulder pads to correct fit, or combine shoulder pads with the minor pattern adjustment. These alternatives camouflage sloping shoulders for more flattering appearance.

Minor Adjustment

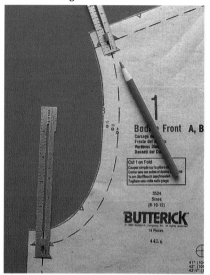

1) Measure *down* from end of shoulder seam to mark the amount seam must be lowered. Lower the side seam at underarm by the same amount. Seams can be lowered a maximum of ½" (1.3 cm).

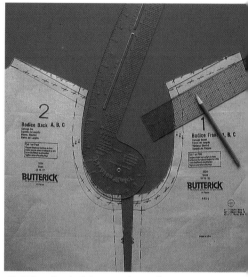

2) Blend stitching and cutting lines. Use straight edge to blend shoulder seams; use curved ruler to blend armhole seam. Make matching adjustment on back and front pattern pieces.

Square Shoulders

Poor fit results when natural shoulders slope less than pattern shoulder seams. Wrinkles form across shoulder area because garment does not rest properly and tends to creep up. If pattern calls for shoulder pads, you may be able to eliminate need for pattern adjustment by using thinner pad than specified.

Minor Adjustment

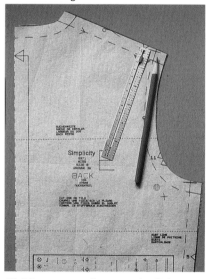

1) Measure *up* from end of the shoulder seam to mark the amount seam must be raised. Mark *up* at underarm seamline to raise it the same amount. Reduce shoulder seam slope a maximum of ½" (1.3 cm) with a minor adjustment.

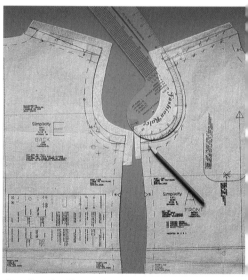

2) Blend adjusted areas into original stitching and cutting lines. Use straight edge to blend the shoulder seam; use curved ruler to blend adjustment at armhole seam. Make matching adjustments on back and front pattern pieces.

Major Adjustment

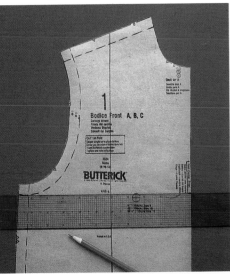

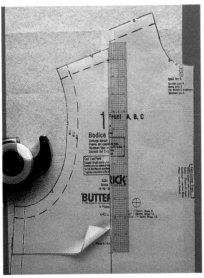

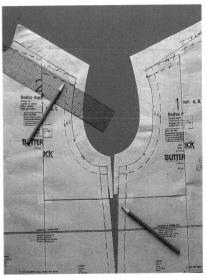

1) Draw adjustment line from midpoint of shoulder seam down, parallel to the grainline. Draw a horizontal line from side seam in, beginning 2" (5 cm) below armhole, at right angle to grainline.

2) Cut pattern on adjustment lines. Slide cut section *down* to lower end of shoulder seam by the amount needed. Lower seam a maximum of 1" (2.5 cm). Tape cut section and pattern to paper.

3) Blend adjusted area into original stitching and cutting lines at shoulder and side seams. Use straight edge when blending. Make matching adjustment on back and front pattern pieces.

Major Adjustment

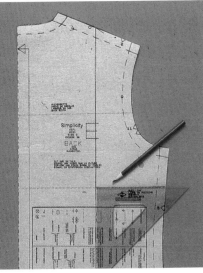

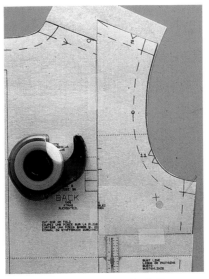

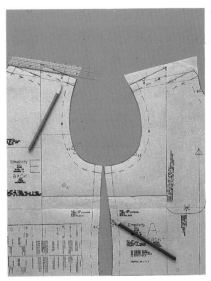

1) Draw vertical adjustment line from midpoint of shoulder seam down, parallel to grainline. Draw a horizontal line from side seam in, beginning 2" (5 cm) below the armhole, at right angle to grainline.

2) Cut pattern on marked lines. Slide cut section *up* to raise end of seam the required amount. Raise seam a maximum of 1½" (3.8 cm) for sizes smaller than 16, and a maximum of 2" (5 cm) for sizes 16 and above. Tape to paper.

3) Blend adjusted area into original stitching and cutting lines at shoulder seam and side seam. Use straight edge when blending. Make matching adjustment on back and front pattern pieces.

Narrow Shoulders

Poor fit results when shoulder seams are too long for natural shoulders. Armhole seam is not at end of shoulder, so upper sleeve droops and wrinkles. The bodice wrinkles near the side; arms feel restricted. Add the appearance of width by using shoulder pads, or combine shoulder pads with a lesser pattern adjustment.

Minor Adjustment

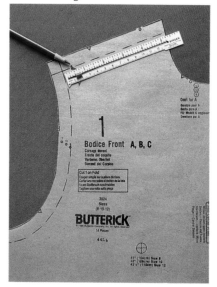

1) Measure *in* from the end of the shoulder seam to mark the amount seam must be shortened. Remove a maximum of 1" (2.5 cm) from sizes 16 and above, and a maximum of ½" (1.3 cm) under size 16.

2) Blend adjusted shoulder seam into original stitching and cutting lines at armhole, using curved ruler. Make matching adjustment on back and front pattern pieces.

Broad Shoulders

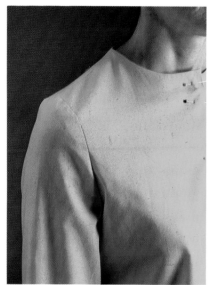

Poor fit on broad shoulders is caused by shoulder seams that are too short. Natural shoulders extend beyond armhole seam into upper sleeve. As a result, set-in sleeve feels too tight, and fabric wrinkles because it is pulled off-grain.

Minor Adjustment

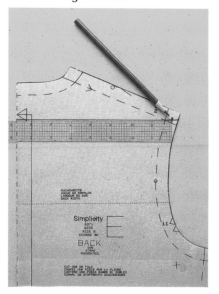

1) Draw a line from the point where shoulder seam and armhole meet to grainline arrow at right angle to grainline. With ruler on this line, measure *out* from end of shoulder seam the amount the seam must be lengthened. Add a maximum of ⅜" (1 cm).

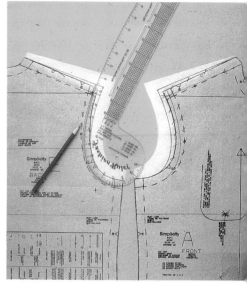

2) Blend lengthened shoulder seam into original shoulder stitching and cutting lines, using straight edge; blend armhole stitching and cutting lines, using curved ruler. Make matching adjustment on back and front.

Major Adjustment

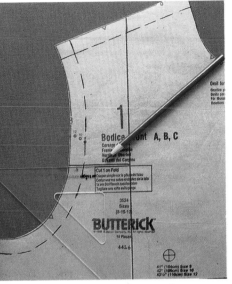

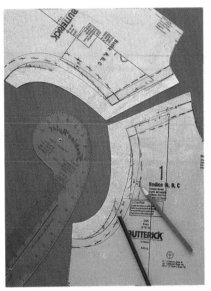

1) Draw adjustment line from midpoint of shoulder seam down, parallel to grainline. Draw second line from armhole seam above notch, at right angle to grainline.

2) Cut pattern on adjustment lines. Slide cut section *in* to shorten the shoulder seam, removing no more than 1½" (3.8 cm). Tape cut sections in place.

3) Blend adjusted area into original stitching and cutting lines at shoulder seam and armholes. Use straight edge for blending shoulder seam; use curved ruler to blend at armhole seam. Make matching adjustment on back and front pattern pieces.

Major Adjustment

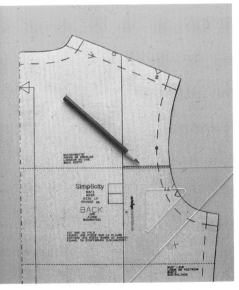

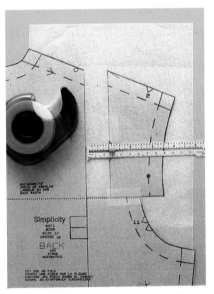

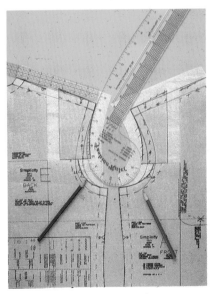

1) Draw adjustment line from midpoint of shoulder seam down, parallel to grainline. Draw second line from armhole seam above notch, at right angle to grainline.

2) Cut pattern on adjustment lines. Slide cut section *out* to lengthen shoulder seam, adding a maximum of 1" (2.5 cm). Tape cut section and pattern to paper.

3) Blend adjusted area into original stitching and cutting lines at shoulder seam and armholes, using straight edge to blend adjustment at shoulder seam; use curved ruler to blend armhole seam. Make matching adjustment on back and front.

Forward Thrust Shoulders

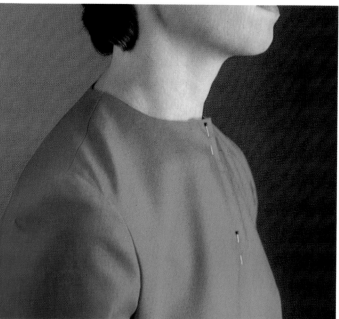

Poor fit occurs when shoulder seams pull toward back of garment because natural shoulders are set in front of earlobes. On garment back, strained fabric causes wrinkles at neckline and back armholes. Set-in sleeves wrinkle and feel uncomfortable.

Minor Adjustment

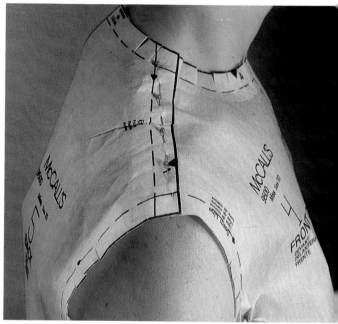

1) Pin-fit pattern, or make trial garment, to determine how much the shoulder seam pulls toward the back. If the amount seems difficult to determine using a tissue pattern, make test garment with 1" (2.5 cm) seams and pin-fit shoulder seams.

Major Adjustment

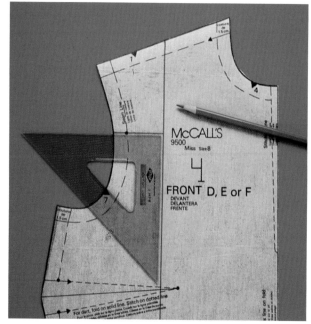

1) Pin-fit as in step 1, above, to determine shoulder seam adjustment. Draw adjustment line from the midpoint of the shoulder seam down, parallel to grainline. Draw second line from the midpoint of armhole, at right angle to grainline. Draw adjustment lines on front and back patterns.

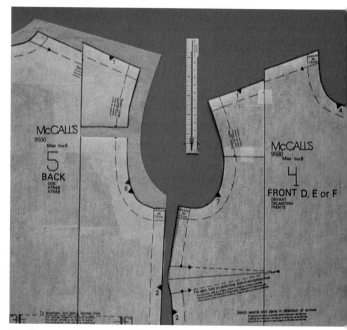

2) Cut on adjustment lines. On front pattern, slide cut section *down* to bring shoulder seam forward the amount required. On back pattern, slide cut section *up* the same amount used to adjust front pattern. Tape cut sections and patterns to paper.

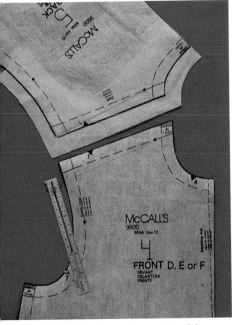

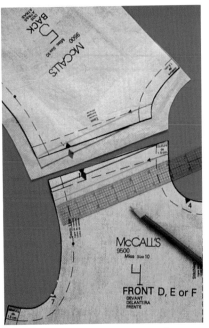

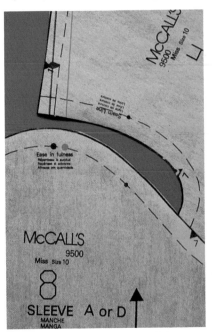

2) Measure *down* from shoulder seamline on front pattern to mark amount seam must be brought forward. Reposition seam maximum of ⅜" (1 cm). Measure *up* from shoulder seamline on back pattern to mark equal adjustment.

3) Blend adjusted portion of shoulder seam into original shoulder seamline on front and back. Use ruler as straight edge when blending.

4) Move dot symbol toward front of sleeve the same amount that shoulder seam was lowered on front pattern. Mark new dot symbol on sleeve pattern so center of sleeve cap lines up with new position of shoulder seam. Single notch indicates front of sleeve.

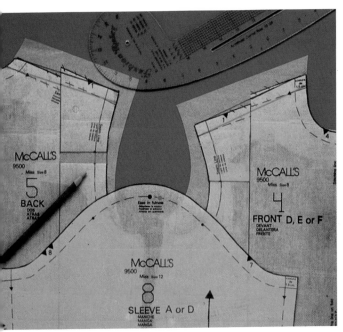

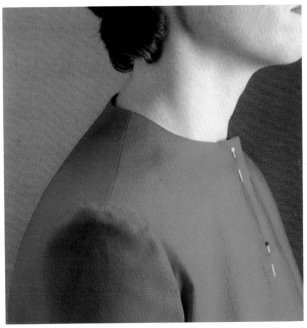

3) Blend adjusted areas into original stitching and cutting lines at shoulder seams and armholes. Use straight edge to blend at shoulder seam; use curved ruler to blend at armhole seam. Mark new dot symbol on sleeve pattern, as in step 4, above.

Corrected fit involves adjusting sleeve cap as well as repositioning shoulder seam toward front on back and front patterns. As a result, shoulder seams now rest properly on natural shoulders. Garment fits comfortably and no longer wrinkles from strain.

Other Shoulder Adjustments

Kimono, dolman, and raglan sleeves have extra ease at the underarm for a relaxed fit, but they still may need adjustments at the shoulder line for width and slope. Whatever the change in a traditional set-in sleeve, the same adjustment should be made when the pattern has other shoulder or sleeve features. The maximum adjustment that should be made is the same as for a major adjustment of a set-in sleeve (pages 57 and 59). Be careful not to overfit; all sleeve styles cut onto the bodice require soft, drapable fabric for good fit. Consider shoulder pads

for minor adjustments. Use the contoured raglan style pad for these fashions.

Raglan sleeve styles are designed with extra ease for relaxed fit. Pin-fit back, front, and sleeve patterns to determine need for pattern adjustments.

Cap, kimono, dolman, and batwing sleeves are derived from traditional set-in sleeves. To compare adjustments, fold set-in sleeve pattern in half at dot on sleeve cap. Pin sleeve cap over front pattern at shoulder seamline. Lay kimono sleeve front pattern on top of set-in sleeve, matching center front lines.

Shoulder Adjustments for Sleeves Cut onto the Bodice

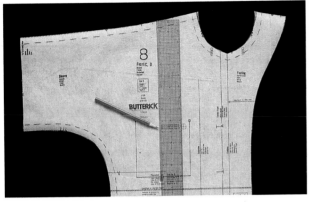

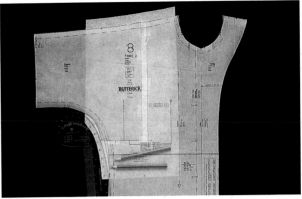

Draw a vertical adjustment line from a point on shoulder seam 3½" to 4" (9 to 10 cm) from neckline to a horizontal line extending from just below the underarm curve. Cut on line to separate sleeve section from bodice. Make matching adjustments on front and back pattern pieces, except for forward thrust shoulders.

Broad shoulders. *Spread* pattern at shoulder seam the amount needed. Place paper under cut edges, and tape in place. Blend stitching and cutting lines at shoulder seam and underarm curve to original bodice. Check new sleeve length.

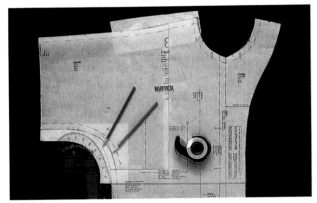

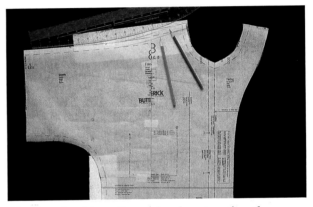

Narrow shoulders. *Lap* pattern at shoulder seam the amount needed. Blend stitching and cutting lines; redraw underarm seam to smooth curve to original bodice. Check new sleeve length.

Sloping shoulders. *Lower* the sleeve section the amount needed. Place paper under cut edges, and tape in place. Blend stitching and cutting lines, and blend underarm curve.

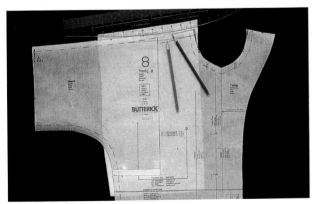

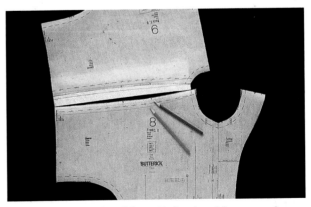

Square shoulders. *Raise* the sleeve section the amount needed. Place paper under cut edges, and tape in place. Blend stitching and cutting lines, and blend underarm curve.

Forward thrust shoulders. *Raise* shoulder seam in back, and *lower* it in front, an equal amount to bring shoulder seam toward front the amount needed to correct the slant. Adjusted seam slants from neck to shoulder; from shoulder to sleeve hem, it is parallel to original seam.

Yokes

Fit patterns that feature yokes or forward shoulder seams by creating a shoulder seam in the yoke and adapting the pattern adjustments used to fit traditional set-in sleeves.

Shoulder Adjustments on Yokes

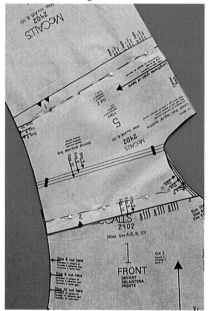

1) Prepare pattern for shoulder adjustments by lapping yoke, front, and back patterns on seamlines. Pin seams together, folding out any gathers, pleats, or eased areas.

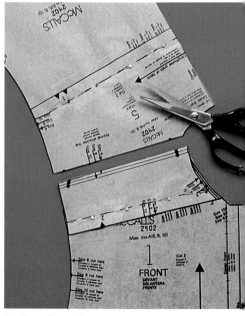

2) Cut the yoke pattern apart on shoulder seamline to separate into back and front sections. If no line is given, draw one by connecting shoulder symbols at yoke neckline and armhole seam.

Raglan Sleeves

Fit a two-piece raglan sleeve pattern by lapping the pattern at seamline where seam starts to straighten out, and adjust the seams in the same way the dart is handled. Avoid over-fitting. For sloping and narrow shoulders, avoid raglan styles, or use shoulder pads rather than dart adjustment, for more flattering fit.

Shoulder Adjustments on Raglan Sleeves

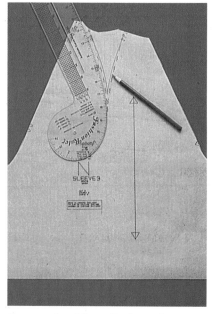

Square shoulders. Reduce slope by drawing new dart stitching lines inside the original lines. This makes dart less contoured.

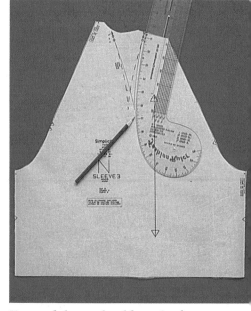

Forward thrust shoulders. Angle dart toward front of sleeve. Determine correct angle for dart by pin-fitting pattern; then check pattern adjustment by trying on garment as you sew.

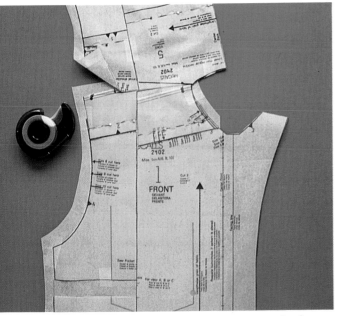

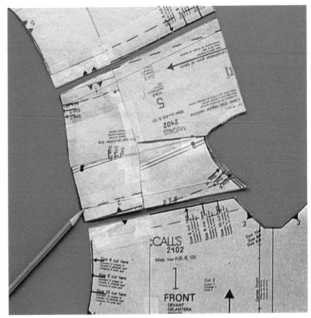

3) Make shoulder seam adjustments as required, with patterns pinned together. Adjustment shown is for square shoulders (pages 56 and 57).

4) Tape yoke sections back together; remove pins to separate front and back patterns. Blend stitching and cutting lines on yoke from original lines at neckline to original lines at armhole. Add seam allowances as necessary to straighten seams on front and back patterns.

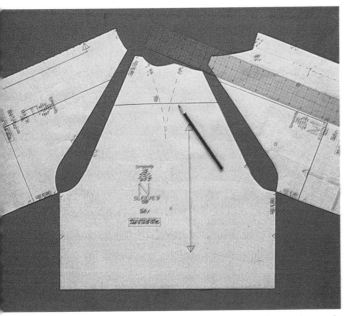

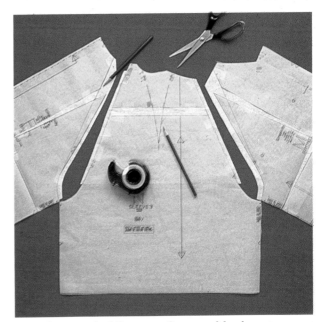

Broad shoulders. 1) Draw a line across sleeve through center of dart, at right angle to grainline. On front and back pattern pieces, measure the same distance from neckline. Draw a line from that mark to 2" (5 cm) below armhole, parallel to grainline. Extend line to side seam.

2) Cut on marked lines; on front and back pattern pieces, cut to, but not through, armhole seam. Place paper under pattern pieces, and spread the amount needed on all three pattern pieces. Redraw dart, and blend stitching and cutting lines at shoulder.

Fitting Necklines, Facings & Collars

The neckline, along with shoulder seams, is a primary fitting area of a garment. This portion of a garment not only frames the face but also influences how the entire garment fits and hangs.

When fitted correctly, a neckline should lie smooth against the body without gaping or wrinkling. Fit the neckline first; then make equivalent adjustments to the collar or facing pattern pieces.

Adjust pattern necklines by small amounts only, working within the standard ⅝" (1.5 cm) seam allowances. Generally, the maximum adjustment is no greater than ⅜" (1 cm) for sizes smaller than 16, and ½" (1.3 cm) for sizes 16 and larger. If you need more than this, consider using another pattern size, especially if adjustments affect the collar. Exceeding the maximum amount complicates adjustments on adjoining pattern pieces.

How to Determine Pattern Adjustments

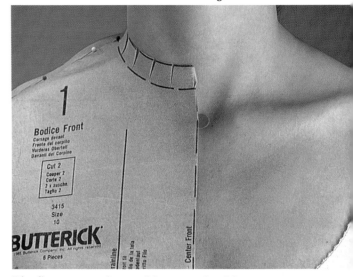

Pin-fit pattern after making any shoulder seam adjustments required. Analyze closely fitted neckline, such as jewel neckline, to see if seamline rests on the collarbone (dot) at front of neck. For better fit, front neck seamline can be raised or lowered.

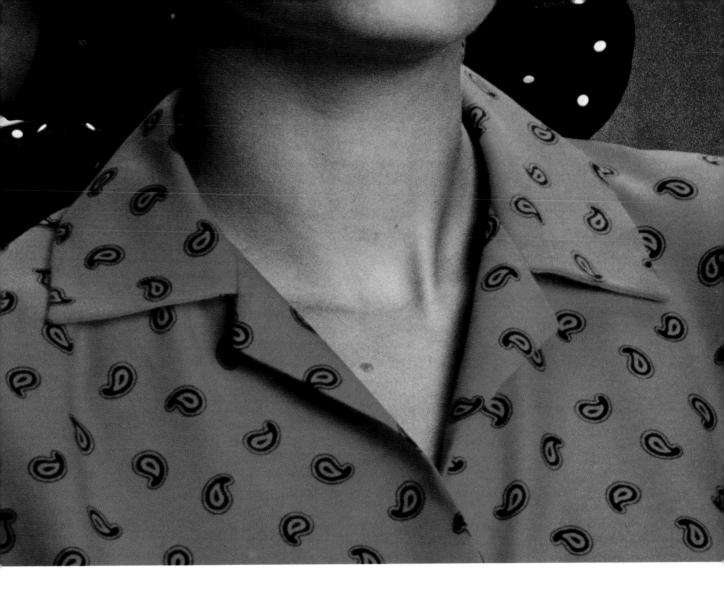

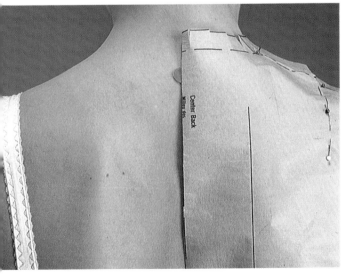

Analyze back neckline fit. Neck seamline at center back should rest on prominent bone (dot) at base of your neck. For better fit, back neck seamline can be raised or lowered.

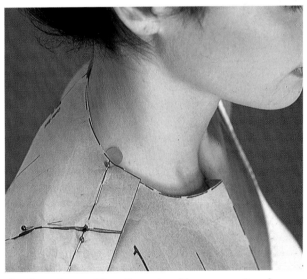

Analyze the neckline fit at shoulder seams. Jewel neckline should rest on neck base in line with earlobe (dot). To find neck base, drop your head and roll it sideways; note where crease forms at side. For a better fit, neckline can be made wider or narrower at shoulder.

Neckline Too High

Poor fit makes neckline feel tight when it rests above neck base. Garment wrinkles because fabric is strained and pulled off-grain. This problem is most common at neck base in front, but can also occur in back. Adjust front or back, using the same method.

Neckline Too Low

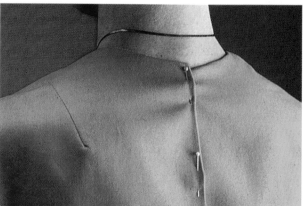

Poor fit results when neckline rests below neck base (chain). Neckline may gap. Fitting problem is most common at neck base in back; use same method to adjust front or back.

How to Lower the Neckline

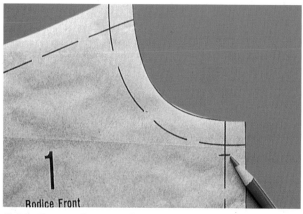

1) Mark new, *lower* neck seamline position with ¼" (6 mm) line at center front or back. Lower the neckline no more than ⅜" (1 cm) if pattern has collar. If it has facing, lower the neckline as needed.

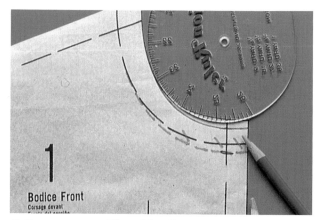

2) Draw new neckline, blending from ¼" (6 mm) line back into original neck seamline, using curved ruler. Line at lower point of neck seamline ensures smooth curve at center front or back.

How to Raise the Neckline

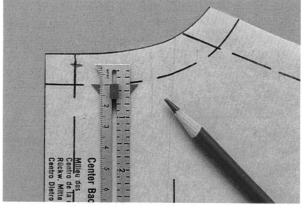

1) Mark new, *higher* neck seamline position with ¼" (6 mm) line at center back or front. Raise neckline no more than ⅜" (1 cm).

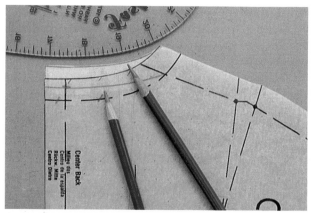

2) Draw new neckline, blending from ¼" (6 mm) line into original seamline. Use curved ruler. Line at lower point of seamline ensures smooth curve.

Neckline Too Wide

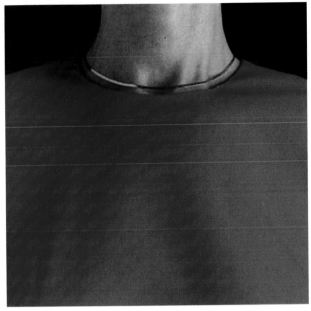

Poor fit in neckline that is too wide makes garment appear too large. Neck seamline falls short of neck base (chain) at shoulders.

Neckline Too Narrow

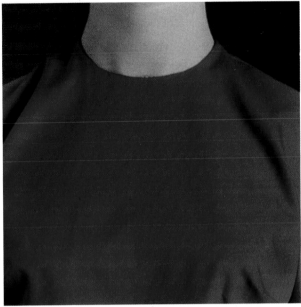

Poor fit in neckline that is too narrow causes diagonal pulls on garment and looks at first like shoulder fitting problem.

How to Adjust the Neckline Width

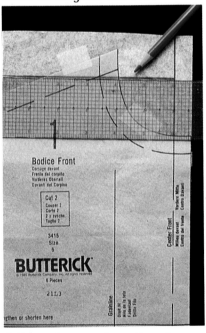

1) **Extend** center front line above neckline. Draw an adjustment line at right angle to the extended center front line, through the point where neck and shoulder seams cross.

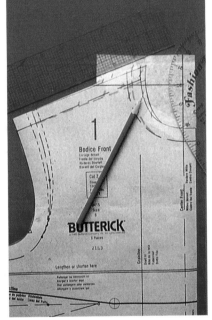

2) **Reduce** neckline width by marking new crossing point for shoulder and neck seams *closer* to center front on adjustment line. Use curved ruler to blend new neckline. Blend shoulder seam from new neckline to armhole. Make adjustment on back and front. Add a maximum of ½" (1.3 cm) to sizes 16 and larger, and ⅜" (1 cm) to smaller sizes.

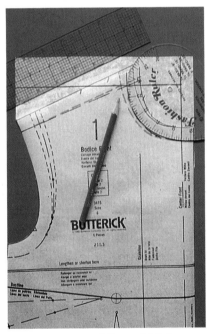

2a) **Increase** neckline width by marking new crossing point for shoulder and neck seams *farther* from center front on adjustment line. Use curved ruler to blend new neckline. Blend shoulder seam from new neckline to armhole. Make adjustment on back and front. Remove maximum of ½" (1.3 cm) from sizes 16 and larger, and ⅜" (1 cm) from smaller sizes.

How to Adjust Facings

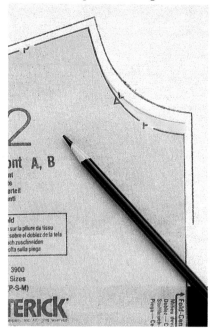

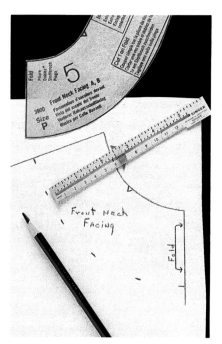

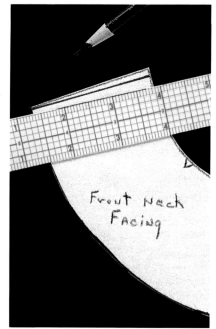

1) Trace new facing pattern if you have made neckline pattern adjustments. Trace adjusted neckline stitching and cutting lines.

2) Measure original facing pattern to determine depth. Draw lower cutting line for facing, using curved ruler.

3) Slant shoulder seamline of facing ⅛" (3 mm) at neckline, tapering to original shoulder seamline at lower edge of facing. For smooth fit, facing must be slightly smaller than neckline.

How to Determine Collar Adjustments

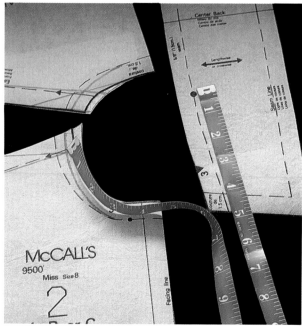

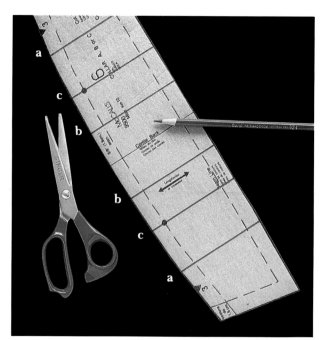

1) Determine adjusted length of neck seamline by measuring neck seamline with tape measure on edge. Measure from shoulder seam to center front, and from shoulder seam to center back. Compare with collar measurements to determine the collar adjustment. Collar pattern has dot to mark shoulder.

2) Draw adjustment line on each side of collar pattern between center front and shoulder dot (**a**) if neckline was adjusted in *front*. If *back* neckline was adjusted, draw adjustment line between center back and shoulder dot (**b**). If neckline *width* was adjusted, draw adjustment line at shoulder dots (**c**). Cut collar pattern apart on lines as needed for adjustment.

How to Adjust Collars

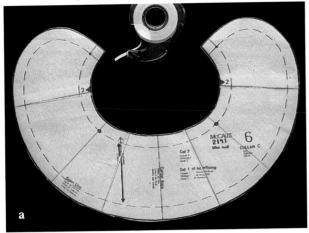

Flat collar. *Spread* collar sections to add amount needed at each adjustment line (**a**), or *lap* collar sections to remove amount needed (**b**). If collar is narrow, keep cut edges parallel. If collar is wide,

spread or lap cut edges at neck seamline, tapering to nothing at outer edge. Tape adjustment in place; blend stitching and cutting lines.

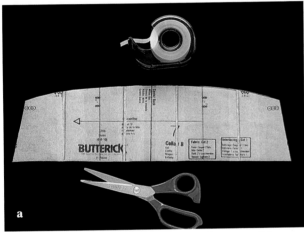

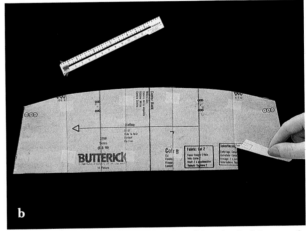

Convertible collar. *Spread* collar sections to add amount needed at each adjustment line (**a**), or *lap* collar sections to remove amount needed (**b**). Keep

cut edges parallel. Tape in place; blend stitching and cutting lines.

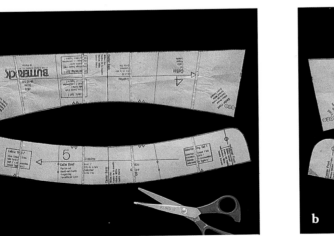

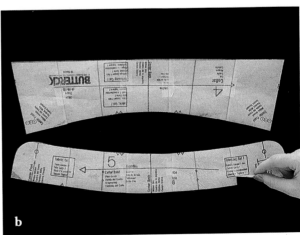

Shirt collar and stand. Use stand pattern to determine collar adjustments as in steps 1 and 2, opposite. *Spread* stand sections to add amount

needed at each adjustment line (**a**), or *lap* stand sections to remove excess (**b**). Keep cut edges parallel. Adjust collar pattern to match stand.

Fitting the Bust

When fitted correctly, the bodice of a garment drapes smoothly over the bust without pulling the side seams forward or the waistline up. Front bodice seams or darts may need to be adjusted to fit your bust size and shape.

If you used your high bust measurement to select a pattern size, you may need to add length and width to the bodice front pattern. If you have selected a pattern featuring relaxed or oversized fit, you can use some of the design ease in the pattern to fit a full bust and make a lesser adjustment.

For an average or small bust, pin-fitting as in step 3 below will determine whether it is necessary to raise or lower darts. Repositioning the darts may be all that is needed to improve pattern fit.

If you make bust adjustments on the pattern beyond simply raising or lowering darts, you may want to test your adjustments by making a bodice fitting shell from the adjusted pattern. Many fitting solutions are easier to visualize in fabric, and this extra step can save time in the long run.

Ease, or extra room, is necessary for comfort at the bustline. Add the minimum amount of ease to your bust measurement, as shown on the chart below, before comparing with the pattern to judge whether pattern adjustments are needed.

The ease amounts given on the chart are general guidelines. At times you may want to fit with more or less ease. For example, thick fabrics require more ease than lightweight ones. Knits require less ease than wovens, and very stretchy knits require no ease at all for formfitting garments. Full figures will be more comfortable with more than the minimum amount of ease.

Minimum Ease

Garment	Minimum Bust Ease
Blouse, dress, jumpsuit	2½" to 3" (6.5 to 7.5 cm)
Unlined jacket	3" to 4" (7.5 to 10 cm)
Lined jacket	3½" to 4½" (9 to 11.5 cm)
Coat	4" to 5" (10 to 12.5 cm)

How to Determine Pattern Adjustments

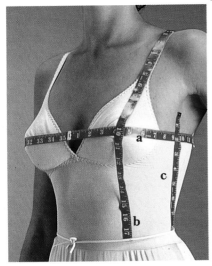

1) Measure bust (**a**) at fullest part, keeping tape measure parallel to floor. Add minimum ease to bust measurement. Measure the front waist length (**b**) from midpoint of shoulder, over bust point, straight down to waist. Measure the side length (**c**) from 1" (2.5 cm) below underarm to waist. Use two fingers under arm to determine distance.

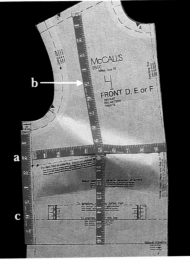

2) Measure pattern at bustline (**a**). Measure bodice front pattern from midpoint of shoulder, over bust point, to waist (**b**). Note any differences to decide if pattern length must be adjusted above waist (pages 48 and 49). Measure side seam of bodice front pattern from underarm to waist (**c**). Note any differences to decide if pattern length must be adjusted.

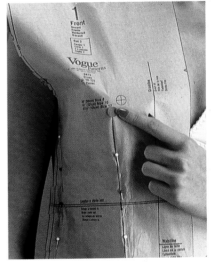

3) Pin-fit pattern to mark the bust point. Note if bust shaping or darts on the pattern should be raised or lowered for good fit. Compare pattern measurement with body measurement plus minimum ease to determine how much width to add for full bust or how much to remove for small bust.

High Bust

Poor fit, when the bust is higher than average, shows in pulls across the fullest part of the bust and in wrinkles under the bust. Dart does not point to fullest part of curve. Underarm dart must be raised; dart from the waistline (if any) needs to be lengthened (page 51).

Low Bust

Poor fit, when the bust is lower than average, shows in pulls across the fullest part of the bust and in wrinkles above the bust. Darts are too high and need to be lowered and shortened (page 51).

How to Raise or Lower Darts

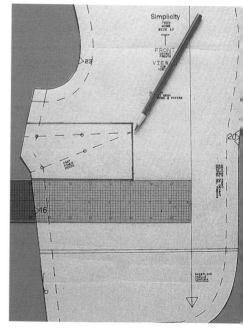

1) Draw horizontal lines on pattern ½" (1.3 cm) above and below the underarm dart, at right angle to grainline. Connect the lines with a vertical line through dart point. Cut out dart on marked lines.

Full Bust

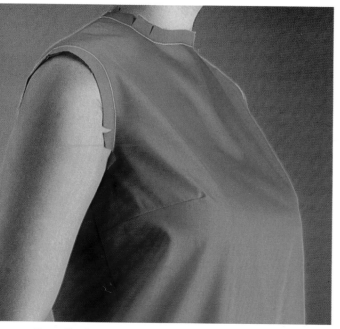

Poor fit shows clearly when pattern is too small for full bust. Bodice rides up in front, and side seams are pulled forward. There is not enough wearing ease across bustline. Add more bodice front length and width by enlarging or creating a dart.

How to Enlarge a Dart

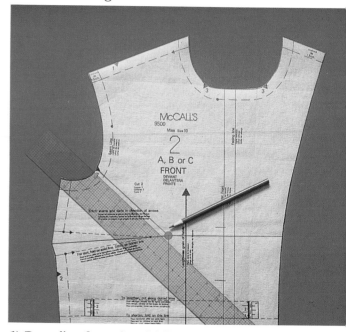

1) Draw line from dart foldline through bust point to center front, at right angle to grainline. Draw a second line from bust point to waist, parallel to grainline. Draw third line from bust point to armhole notch.

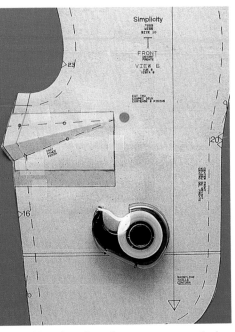

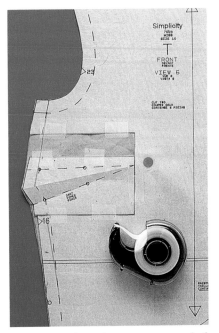

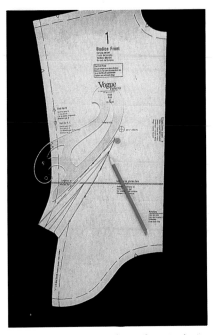

2) Raise dart the amount needed for a high bust. Position dart so that it points to the bust point (dot) or fullest part of figure. Place paper under pattern. Tape cut edges in place, keeping edges even. Redraw side seam.

2a) Lower dart the amount needed for a low bust. Position dart so that it points to the bust point (dot) or fullest part of figure. Place paper under pattern. Tape cut edges in place, keeping edges even. Redraw side seam.

Diagonal dart requires change in direction so that it points to bust point. Mark new dart point on pattern. Redraw dart, connecting side seam ends of the dart and new dart point.

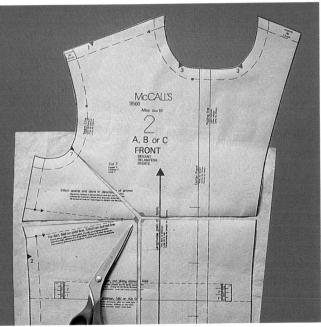

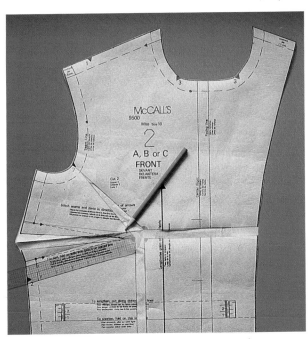

2) Cut pattern from waist to bust point and from bust point up to, but not through, armhole notch. Cut center line of dart to, but not through, bust point. Cut from center front to bust point.

3) Finish adjustment as for adding a bust dart, pages 76 and 77, steps 3 to 6.

How to Add a Bust Dart

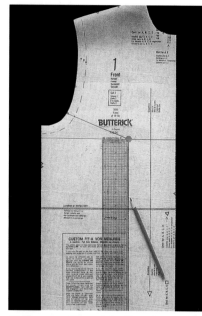 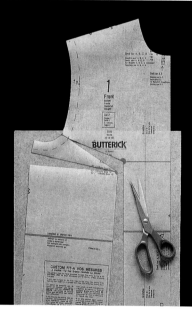 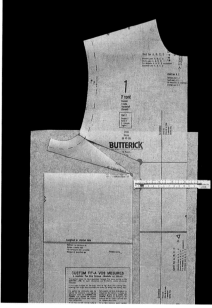

1) Draw adjustment line from side seam through bust point to center front, at right angle to grainline. Draw second line from bust point to armhole notch. Draw third line from bust point to waist seamline or hem, parallel to grainline.

2) Cut pattern on first adjustment line from side seam to, but not through, bust point. Cut on second line from waist to bust point, then from bust point to armhole seam.

3) Spread pattern at bustline half the required amount. Standard amount of width is ½" (1.3 cm) for C cup, ¾" (2 cm) for D cup, and 1¼" (3.2 cm) or more for cup sizes larger than D. Keep sides of vertical slash parallel. Bust dart will open as the pattern is spread.

How to Fit a Full Bust without Darts

 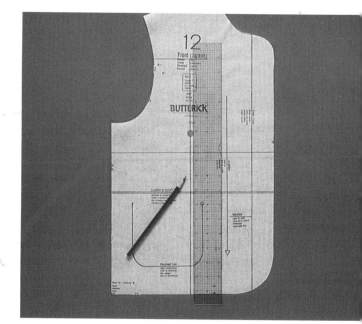

Accommodate full bust on less closely fitted pattern styles by making an adjustment that does not create a dart. This method can be used to increase the pattern a limited amount. Exceeding the maximum adjustment distorts the fabric grain at the lower edge of the garment. This adjustment is not appropriate on plaids, checks, or stripes.

1) Draw line across bodice front midway between armhole notch and shoulder seam, at right angle to grainline. Draw second line 2" to 4" (5 to 10 cm) below armhole, at right angle to grainline. Draw third line through bust point, parallel to grainline to connect first two lines; extend line to lower edge.

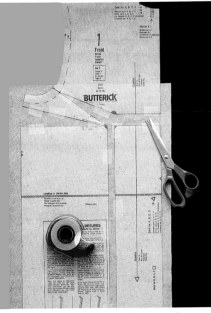

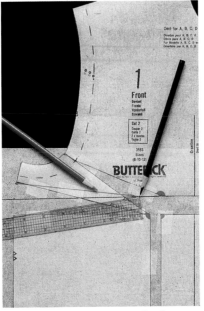

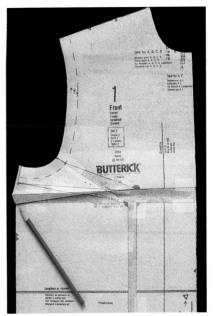

4) Cut from center front to bust point. Slide center front section *down* so waist seamline matches lower edge of side front section. Tape to paper.

5) Draw dart foldline to the bust point, beginning at side seam in center of added area. Mark dart stitching lines from the side seam to 1" (2.5 cm) from the bust point for sizes smaller than 16, or 2" to 2½" (5 to 6.5 cm) from bust point for sizes 16 and larger.

6) Fold out the dart to blend stitching and cutting lines at side seam. Blend stitching and cutting lines at lower edge.

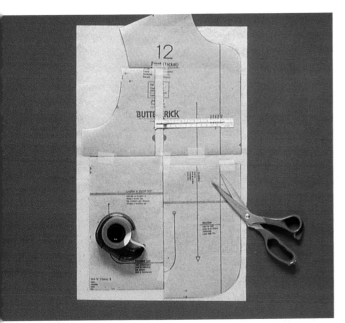

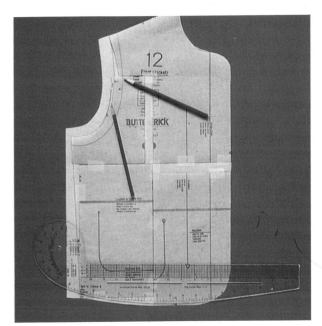

2) Cut pattern on adjustment lines. Slide armhole portion *out* a maximum of ¾" (2 cm) to add total of 1½" (3.8 cm) to bodice width. Slide center front waist section *down* no more than 2" (5 cm) to add bodice length. Tape to paper.

3) Blend stitching and cutting lines at armhole and side seams. Use curved ruler to blend lower cutting line from the center front, tapering back to the original side seam.

Gaping Armhole

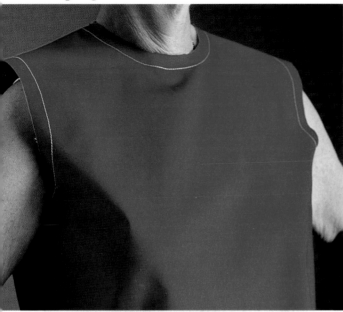

Poor fit results in excess gaping fabric at armhole, caused by combination of full bust and narrow shoulders, even though the bust dart may fit correctly. Fitting problem is typical of, but not limited to, half-size figure type.

Minor Adjustment

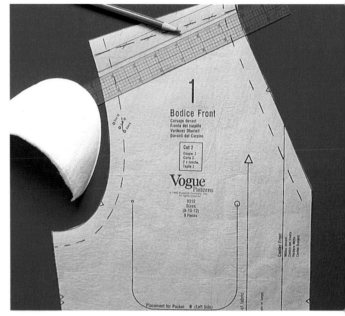

Remove up to ¾" (2 cm) by marking lower shoulder seamline on front bodice only. Taper stitching and cutting lines back into original shoulder seamline at neck edge, using straight edge. Shoulder pads may also be used for minor adjustment.

Small Bust

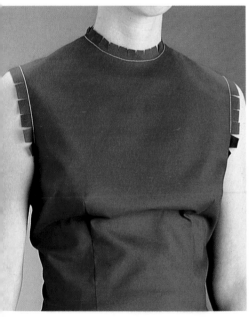

Poor fit makes garment look baggy, because bodice is too wide and long for small bust. Standard pattern darts need to be reduced or eliminated, because they are too deep and shapely for small bust contours.

Minor Adjustment

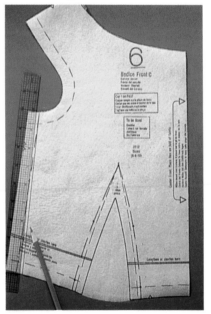

Draw new dart stitching lines inside original lines. Remove up to ⅜" (1 cm) from dart to reduce a total of ¾" (2 cm). Remove same amount from bodice front side seam to maintain original waist size. Blend side seam cutting lines.

How to Eliminate a Bust Dart

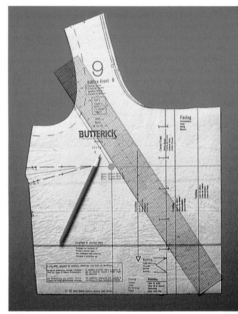

1) Draw line from dart foldline to bust point. Extend line from bust point to center front, at right angle to grainline. Draw second line from bust point to waist, parallel to grainline. Draw third line from bust point to armhole notch.

Major Adjustment

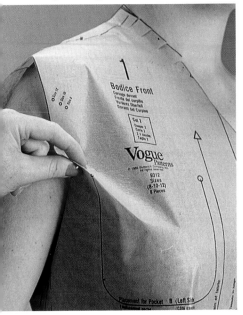

1) Pin-fit pattern, pinning in a dart to correct gaping armhole.

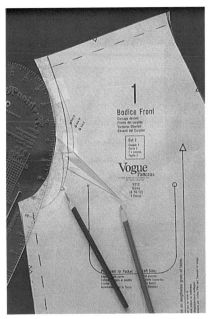

2) Mark dart stitching lines on bodice front pattern. Fold out dart to blend cutting line.

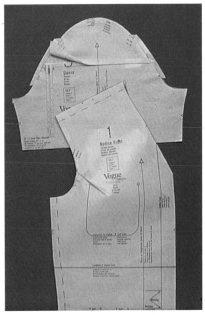

3) Measure armhole and sleeve cap between notches. If ease in sleeve is more than 1½" (3.8 cm), cut pattern across top of cap; overlap to remove an amount equal to depth of dart.

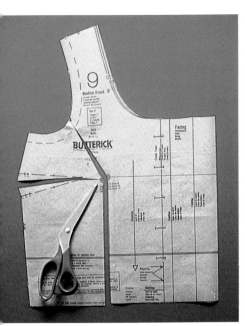

2) Cut on adjustment line from waist to bust point and from bust point to, but not through, armhole notch. Cut dart foldline to, but not through, bust point.

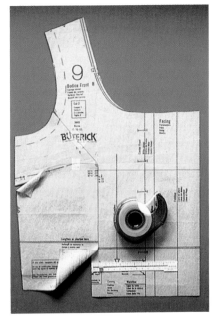

3) Slide side front pattern *in* to remove half the amount of bodice width needed and *up* to remove excess front bodice length. Keep vertical slash parallel to center front line. Standard amount of width to remove is ½" (1.3 cm) or more for cup size A or smaller. Tape in place.

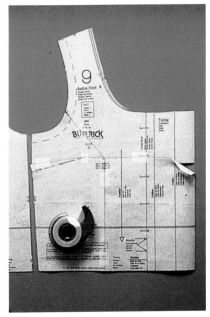

4) Cut on horizontal line, and raise center front section until waistline is even. Compare adjusted length of side seam on front bodice with length of side seam on back bodice. If side seams are the same length, dart has been eliminated.

Princess Seams

Patterns with princess seams make bust fitting easy. The seams divide the bodice front into three or more panels. This provides ample opportunity for making pattern adjustments in the seam allowances.

There are two basic types of princess seams. The seams of one originate at the armhole. The seams of the other originate at the shoulder seam. For either type, lap the bodice front and bodice side panels together on the seamline to see where the seam shapes the bustline. Pin-fit the pattern to determine and mark the bust point. Adjust the shaping to fit your bust contours.

How to Raise or Lower Bust Fullness

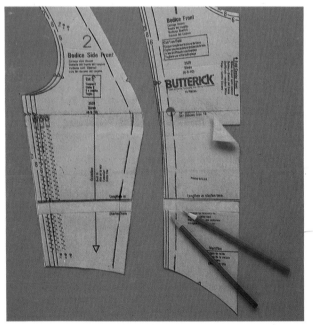

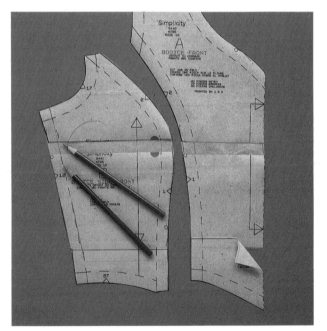

High bust. Draw adjustment line through bust point (dot) at right angle to grainline. Cut on line; *lap* pattern the amount needed. To compensate for change in length, cut pattern on adjustment line below bustline. *Spread* pattern the same amount bust point was raised. Make matching adjustment on adjoining pattern.

Low bust. Draw adjustment line through bust point (dot) at right angle to grainline. Cut on line; *spread* pattern the amount needed. To compensate for change in length, cut pattern on adjustment line below bustline. *Lap* pattern the same amount bust point was lowered. Make matching adjustment on adjoining pattern.

How to Fit a Full Bust

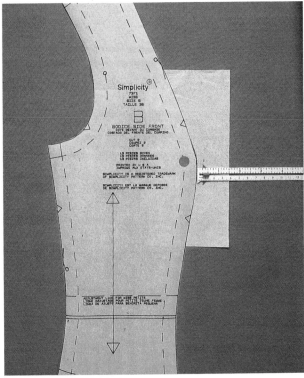

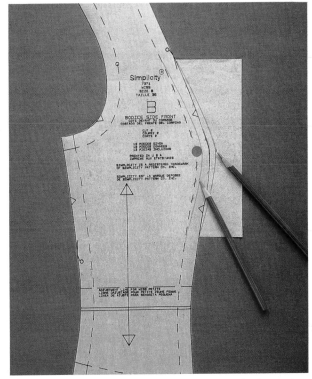

1) Measure out from cutting line at fullest part of bustline curve, adding ¼" (6 mm) for each bra cup size larger than B.

2) Blend stitching and cutting lines from the increase mark to points 4" (10 cm) above and 4" (10 cm) below the bustline.

How to Fit a Small Bust

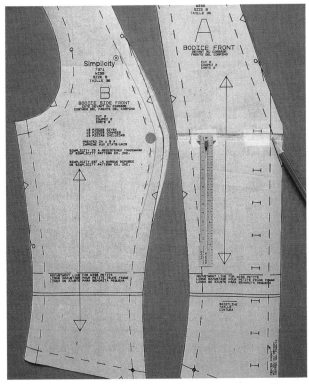

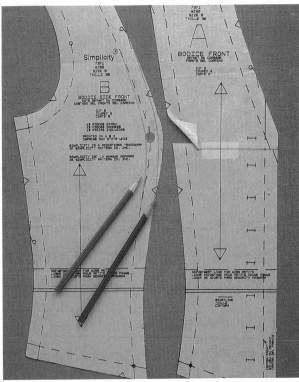

3) Cut center front pattern apart between notches, and lengthen ¼" (6 mm) for each bra cup size that pattern is being increased.

Reverse the adjustment that was made for a full bust; remove ¼" (6 mm) from side front seam, and lap ¼" (6 mm) in center section.

Fitting the Back

Good fit across the back of a garment contributes to wearing comfort. When the arms are straight at the sides, a well-fitted garment fits smoothly across the back. When the arms are folded in front, the garment feels comfortable, and neither the fabric nor the armhole seams are strained.

Many back fitting problems are the result of posture or bone structure variations. For a narrow or broad back, adjust the back bodice width for better fit. For a rounded back, add shoulder darts and back bodice length at center back to accommodate the contours. For an extremely rounded back, often called a dowager's hump, add neckline darts to shape the back bodice for a wrinkle-free appearance.

Ease, or extra room, is necessary for comfort across the back of a garment. Add the amount of ease from the chart at right to the back measurement to judge whether pattern adjustments are needed, and if so, how much.

The minimum ease amounts given are general guidelines; however, at times you may want to fit patterns with more or less ease. Sleeveless garments require less ease across the upper back than those with sleeves. Thick fabrics require more ease than thin ones, and knits require less ease than wovens. Very stretchy knits require no ease at all for form-fitting garments. A large size or full figure may be more comfortable with more ease.

Minimum Ease

Garment	Minimum Back Ease
Blouse, dress, sleeveless jumpsuit	½" to 1" (1.3 to 2.5 cm)
Jumpsuit with sleeves	1" (2.5 cm)
Jacket	1" to 1½" (2.5 to 3.8 cm)
Coat	1" to 2" (2.5 to 5 cm)

How to Determine Pattern Adjustments

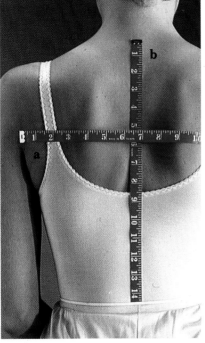

1) Measure back width (**a**) from arm crease to arm crease, 4" to 6" (10 to 15 cm) below prominent bone at base of neck. Add minimum ease. Measure back waist length (**b**) from prominent bone at back of neck to waist. Compare with back waist length given on pattern envelope to determine adjustments.

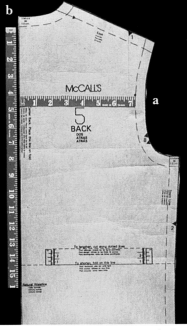

2) Measure pattern from armhole seam to the center back (**a**) at the same distance below neck base as measured in step 1. Double this measurement for total back bodice width; compare with body measurement plus ease. Measure back waist length (**b**); compare with measurement on pattern envelope to determine amount of ease or blousing, if any.

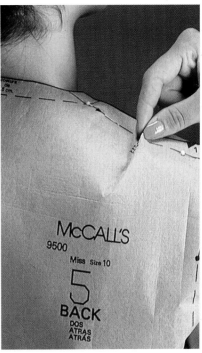

3) Pin-fit pattern after width and length have been adjusted. Pin-fit to determine dart placement for rounded back, dowager's hump, or protruding shoulder blades. These adjustments may be difficult to measure because they correspond to individual figure contours.

Rounded Back

Poor fit causes bodice to wrinkle, because more length is needed over rounded back. Garment rides up at back waistline, causing hem to drape unevenly in back. Protruding shoulder blades create horizontal wrinkles below back neckline.

Extremely High Rounded Back

Poor fit stems from rounded posture, forming protrusion (dowager's hump) below neck base in back. Neckline stands away from neck in the back and binds in the front. Garment needs a dart at neckline to fit high, rounded back contour.

How to Add Length for a Rounded Back

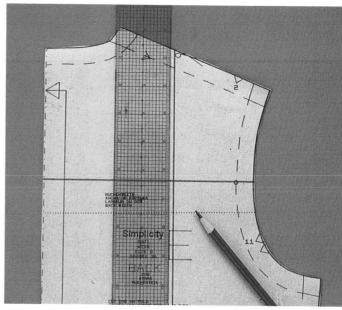
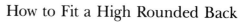

1) Draw adjustment line from center back about 4" (10 cm) below neck to armhole, at right angle to grainline. Draw second line from center of shoulder seam or center of shoulder dart (if any) down to waistline, parallel to grainline.

How to Fit a High Rounded Back

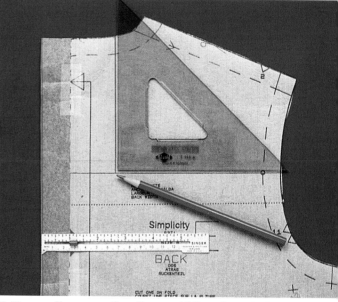

1) Draw adjustment line from middle of armhole to center back, at right angle to grainline. Draw second line from center of neck seamline to first line, parallel to grainline. If pattern has no center back seam, create one by adding up to 1½" (3.8 cm) seam allowance to center back fold.

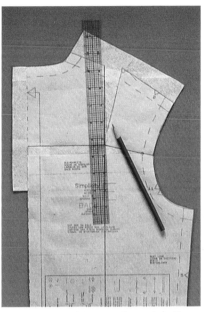

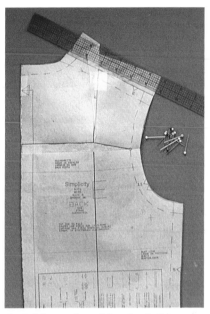

2) Cut pattern on first adjustment line, up to armhole seamline. Cut on second adjustment line up to, but not through, first line. Slide upper section *up* to add length at center back, tapering to nothing at armhole. Tilt armhole section *out* to create or increase shoulder dart.

3) Blend stitching and cutting lines at center back. Draw stitching lines to create the new shoulder dart or increase the existing dart.

4) Fold out dart; blend stitching and cutting lines at shoulder seam. Shorten or lengthen dart, if necessary, to fit protruding shoulder blades (page 51).

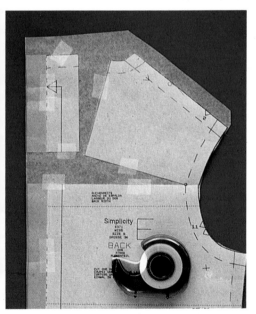

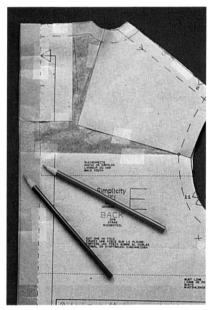

2) Cut pattern on first adjustment line, up to armhole seamline. Cut pattern on second adjustment line. Slide center back section *up* to add length needed. Slide shoulder section *out* to create neckline dart. Tape paper underneath.

3) Blend stitching and cutting lines at center back. Draw neckline dart. Fold out dart, and blend stitching and cutting lines at neckline seam.

4) Adjust shape and length of dart during trial fitting of garment or by pin-fitting pattern. If garment fabric is lightweight, dart can be converted to gathers. Take in or let out center back seam as needed. Adjust facing or collar to fit neckline (pages 70 and 71).

Fitting Sleeves

Judge a well-fitted sleeve by its length and width. The hem or cuff of a full-length blouse or dress sleeve should hit the center of the wristbone when the arm is slightly bent. If the sleeve is gathered at the cap or the cuff, allow enough extra length for graceful blousing. Coat sleeves should be long enough to cover sleeves of garments that are worn underneath. Jacket sleeves should be slightly shorter so the blouse or dress sleeve shows. If a garment requires shoulder pads, wear them when fitting sleeves, because pads raise the shoulders, shortening the sleeve length.

Sleeves must be wide enough to fit around the upper arm without strain. To remove any wrinkles, adjust the upper sleeve width or redistribute the ease in the sleeve cap. When your arm is hanging down in a relaxed position, the sleeve should drape slightly forward.

Ease, or extra room, is necessary for sleeves to fit upper arms comfortably. To judge whether pattern adjustments are needed, add minimum ease from the chart at right to the upper arm measurement. The ease amounts given are guidelines, but at times you may want to fit sleeves with a greater or lesser amount of ease. For example, traditional set-in sleeves may fit so closely that you may have to adjust the ease to suit the garment fabric. Thick fabrics require more ease than thin ones, and knits require less than wovens. Very stretchy knits require no ease for formfitting garments. Also, large sizes or full upper arms will be more comfortable with more than minimum ease.

If your pattern has shirt, pouffed, or kimono sleeves, the sleeve pattern will have design ease in addition to minimum ease because of the fuller cut. You can often avoid pattern adjustments at the upper arm by selecting such sleeve styles.

Minimum Ease

Garment	Minimum Upper Arm Ease
Blouse	1" to 1½" (2.5 to 3.8 cm)
Dress, jumpsuit	1½" to 2" (3.8 to 5 cm)
Unlined jacket	3" to 4" (7.5 to 10 cm)
Lined jacket	3" to 4½" (7.5 to 11.5 cm)
Coat	4" to 5½" (10 to 14 cm)

How to Determine Pattern Adjustments

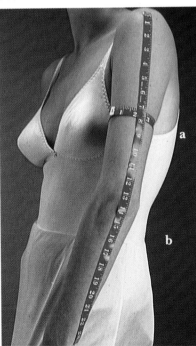

1) **Measure** upper arm (**a**). Add minimum ease from chart above. Measure arm length (**b**) from shoulder to wrist with arm slightly bent. Note the shoulder-to-elbow distance if sewing a set-in sleeve fitted with darts, shaped seams, or eased fabric at elbow.

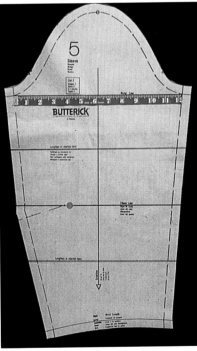

2) **Measure** sleeve pattern from seam to seam at underarm. Compare with upper arm measurement plus minimum ease to decide if width of the sleeve pattern needs an adjustment. Dot marks location of elbow.

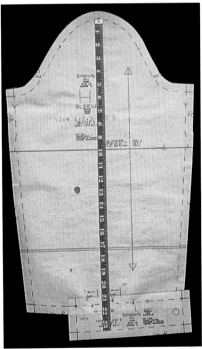

3) **Measure** pattern from stitching line at center of sleeve cap to hem. If sleeve has cuff, add finished width of cuff. Compare with arm length to determine basic length adjustments. If sleeve is fitted at elbow, divide adjustment above and below the elbow.

Full Upper Arm

Poor fit occurs when there is too little ease in sleeve at upper arm. Wrinkles form because sleeve is too tight. This fitting problem is most common with traditional set-in sleeves.

Minor Adjustment

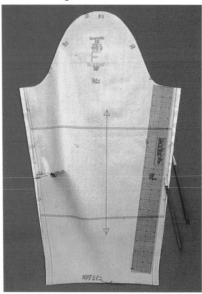

Draw new stitching lines on sleeve pattern at underarm to add up to ⅜" (1 cm) at each seam allowance for total of ¾" (2 cm). Blend stitching and cutting lines to lower edge. Ease extra sleeve fabric into garment armhole below notches.

Major Adjustment

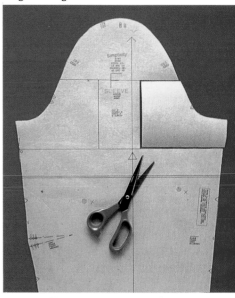

1) Draw line across pattern about 1" (2.5 cm) above notches, at right angle to grainline. Draw second line about 2" (10 cm) below underarm, parallel to first line. Divide sleeve cap into three equal parts with the two lines parallel to grainline. Cut pattern apart on adjustment lines.

Thin Upper Arm

Poor fit results from too much ease in sleeves, causing fabric to droop and form folds in upper arm area, especially if the fabric is lightweight or clinging. To correct this problem, reverse the minor adjustment for full upper arm, above.

Avoid calling attention to thin upper arms by over-adjusting. Instead, raise shoulder slightly as for square shoulder adjustment (page 56), and use shoulder pads to support sleeve caps.

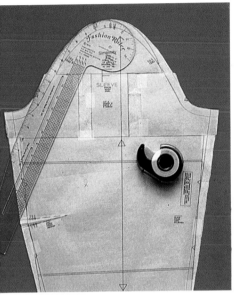

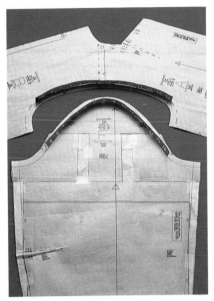

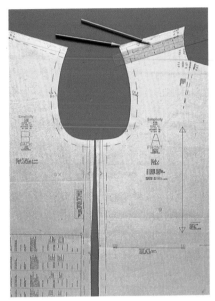

2) Spread sleeve cap sections equally to add needed width, adding maximum of 1½" (3.8 cm) at each cut for total of 3" (7.5 cm). Tape paper underneath. Blend stitching and cutting lines with curved ruler.

3) Measure bodice front and back armhole between notches; measure sleeve cap between notches. Then compare measurements. Sleeve cap should be no more than 1" (2.5 cm) longer on firm fabrics, such as corduroy, denim, and synthetic suede, or 1½" to 2" (3.8 to 5 cm) longer on soft fabrics, such as knits and loose weaves.

4) Make minor adjustments at shoulder and underarm seams of front and back to compensate for fuller sleeve cap. Add half the amount needed at each place. Add shoulder pads.

Sleeve Length Adjustments

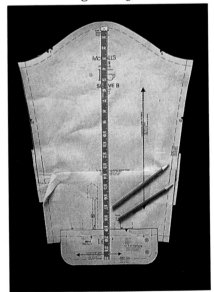

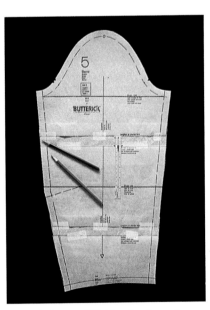

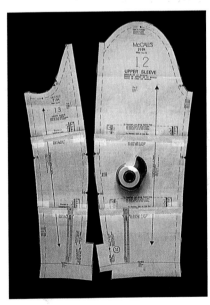

Shirt sleeve. Cut pattern on printed adjustment line. Shorten sleeve by overlapping cut edges, Lengthen by spreading cut edges, taping paper underneath to bridge gap. Blend stitching and cutting lines. Remember to take into account finished depth of cuff.

Fitted sleeve. Divide the length adjustment above and below elbow to ensure that elbow shaping is in correct position. Cut pattern on printed adjustment line above and below elbow, at right angle to grainline. Shorten or lengthen as for shirt sleeve, left.

Two-piece sleeve. Eased area between notches on outer seam fits sleeve to elbow. Divide length adjustment above and below elbow, as for fitted sleeve, left. Make matching length adjustments on both sleeve sections.

Fitting the Waist & Abdomen

Although a waistband or waistline should fit snugly, it must be slightly larger than your waist for good fit. For wearing comfort, a waistband should be from ½" to ¾" (1.3 to 2 cm) larger than your actual waist measurement for pattern sizes smaller than 16. For size 16 or larger, make the waistband at least 1" (2.5 cm) larger than your waist. Apply the same fitting guidelines to garments with faced waistlines or waistline seams.

One indication of good waist fit is the way the side seams hang. They should hang straight, without being pulled to the front or the back. A full abdomen

will make the waist measurement larger in the front than the back. On a swayback posture the body is shorter in the center back than the average, making the back waistline measurement smaller.

Adjustments for full abdomen and swayback should be determined and made at the same time that the waist is taken into consideration. For a prominent abdomen, adjust the front pattern pieces and shift the side seams toward the back to add room in the front where it is needed. For a swayback posture, adjust only the back pattern pieces to contour them to your personal shape.

How to Determine Pattern Adjustments

1) Measure your waist. Compare with the waist measurement for your pattern size. Minimum wearing ease is included in the pattern, so adjust the pattern accordingly, enlarging or reducing as needed.

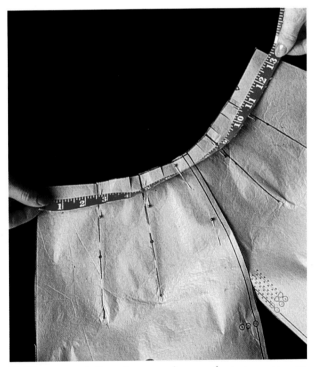

2) Pin out waistline darts, tucks, or pleats to measure pattern to compare with body measurements plus ease. Measure at the waistline seam; on a garment without a waistline seam, measure at the waistline mark at the narrowest part of the waistline area. Double the pattern measurement to compare with your waist measurement.

Small Waist

Poor fit has waistline or waistband that is too large, although garment fits at hips and bust. A dress with a waistline seam is baggy, with loose vertical folds at the waist. On a skirt or pants, waistband stands away from waist and tends to slide down.

Minor Adjustment

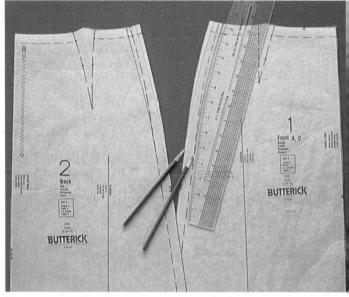

Remove one-fourth the amount needed at each seam. Maximum of ⅜" (1 cm) per seam allowance may be removed from pattern sizes smaller than 16. From sizes 16 and larger, remove maximum of ⅝" (1.5 cm). Blend stitching and cutting lines, using curved ruler. On dart-fitted skirts or pants, do not make darts deeper to reduce waistline unless additional garment contouring is needed to fit broad curvy hips or full round seat. Adjust adjoining pattern pieces as on page 98.

Large Waist

Poor fit is indicated by horizontal wrinkles near the waist, which cause the waistline of a dress to rise. A waistband on skirt or pants creases from strain. Wrinkles fan out from waist or form horizontal folds below waistband.

Minor Adjustment

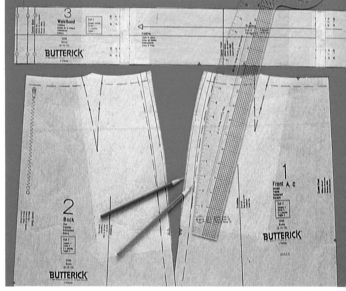

Add one-fourth the amount needed at each seam, adding up to ⅜" (1 cm) per seam allowance for total of ¾" (2 cm) per seam. On dart-fitted skirts, each dart can be reduced up to ¼" (6 mm) to enlarge waistline further. Blend stitching and cutting lines, using curved ruler. Adjust adjoining waistband, facing, or bodice patterns as on page 98.

Major Adjustment

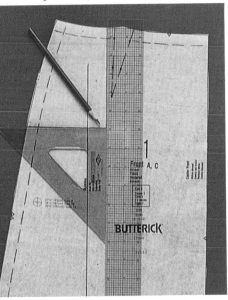

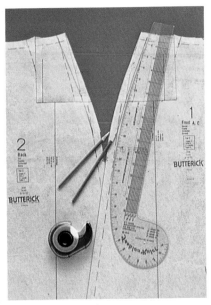

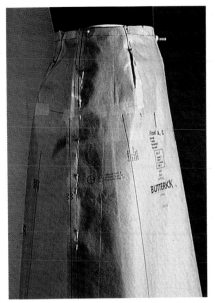

1) Draw a line 5" to 6" (12.5 to 15 cm) long from waist seam midway between side seam and center front, parallel to grainline. Draw second line from bottom of first line to side seam, at right angle to grainline. Cut on adjustment lines.

2) Slide section *in* to remove up to 1" (2.5 cm) from waist seam. Tape paper underneath. Blend stitching and cutting lines. Make matching adjustment on back, removing up to 2" (5 cm) from each seam for a total reduction of 4" (10 cm).

3) Pin-fit pattern to check position of waistline darts. It may be necessary to move darts closer to center front and back for good fit. To reposition dart, see page 74. Adjust adjoining waistband, facing, or bodice patterns as on page 98.

Major Adjustment

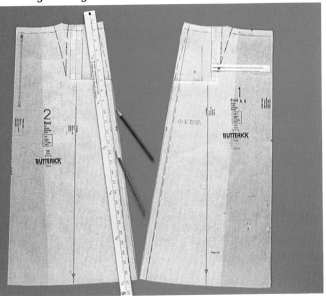

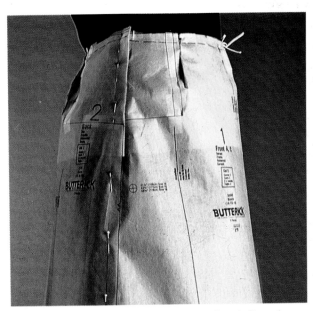

1) Draw adjustment lines and cut pattern as in step 1 for small waist, above. Slide section *out* up to 1" (2.5 cm). Tape paper underneath. Blend stitching and cutting lines to waist, using curved ruler, and to hem, using straight edge. Make matching adjustment on back pattern, adding up to 2" (5 cm) per seam for total of 4" (10 cm).

2) Pin-fit pattern to check position of waistline darts. It may be necessary to move them closer to side seams for better fit. To reposition darts, see page 74. Adjust adjoining waistband, facing, or bodice sections as on page 98.

Prominent Abdomen

Poor fit is indicated by horizontal wrinkles across the front below the waistline. Diagonal wrinkles from abdomen to sides pull side seams forward. Waistline and hemline may ride up. Extra length and width are needed at center front.

Minor Adjustment

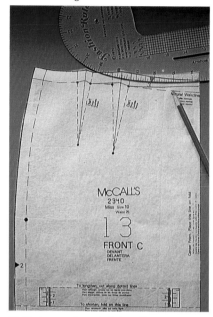

1) Raise waist stitching line on front skirt or pants pattern up to ⅜" (1 cm) at center front to add more length. Fold out darts, and blend stitching and cutting lines, using curved ruler.

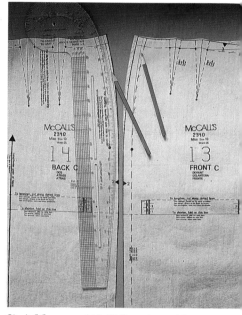

2) Add up to ½" (1.3 cm) at side seam of the front pattern piece. Remove same amount from back pattern piece to maintain the waist circumference. To further improve fit, convert front darts to gathers or unpressed pleats.

Flat Abdomen

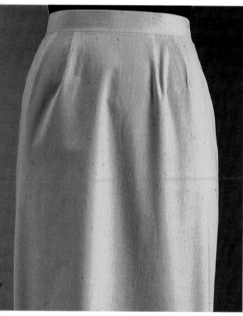

Poor fit is indicated by vertical wrinkles and excess fabric at center front. Hipbones may protrude. Darts are poorly located and too deep for flat abdomen contour.

Adjustments for Flat Abdomen

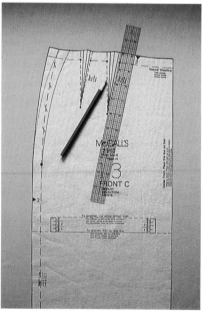

Redraw shallower darts by removing an equal amount on each side of dart foldline. To restore the original waistline measurement, remove the same amount from side seam, blending from a point on waistline seam to hipline with curved ruler.

Move darts closer to side seam for prominent hipbones. Cut out dart as for raising or lowering bust dart (pages 76 and 77), and slide it to correct position after pin-fitting pattern. Fold out dart, and blend waistline stitching and cutting lines, using curved ruler.

Major Adjustment

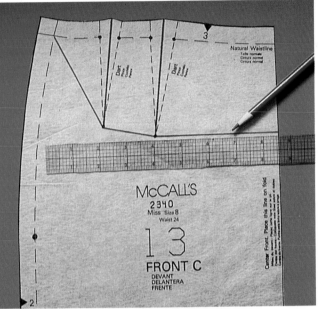

1) Draw diagonal adjustment lines on pattern from intersection of side seam and waistline seam through dart points, extending at right angle to center front. Cut on line. Cut on dart foldline to, but not through, dart point.

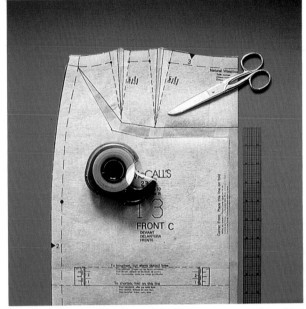

2) Slide center section *up* the amount needed and *out* half the amount needed, opening darts and diagonal slash. Extend center front line from new position to hemline. Darts can also be converted to gathers or unpressed pleats. Blend stitching and cutting lines at waistline.

Swayback

Poor fit is caused by posture variation; area directly beneath waist in back looks scooped, indicating that garment is too long between waist and hips at center back. Wrinkles that form are deeper at center back than at sides. Darts emphasize fitting problem by contouring garment to wrong shape.

Adjustment for Swayback

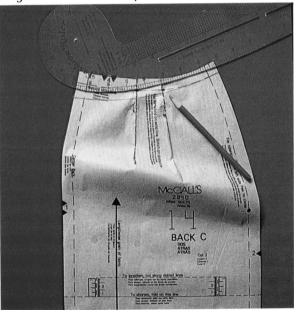

Lower the waist stitching line on the back skirt pattern up to ¾" (2 cm). Blend stitching and cutting lines, using curved ruler. To further improve fit, convert any back darts to gathers for a softer look. Greater adjustment than this indicates the need for a flat seat adjustment (pages 108 and 109).

Adjusting Waistband, Facing & Bodice

If you have adjusted the skirt or pants pattern pieces for better waistline fit, adjust the adjoining pattern pieces accordingly. As a rule, make a matching adjustment at the same place on the waistband, facing, or bodice pattern as made on the skirt or pants. To find the correct location for the change, use the pattern symbols that indicate side seams and center front and back.

How to Adjust a Waistband or Waist Facing

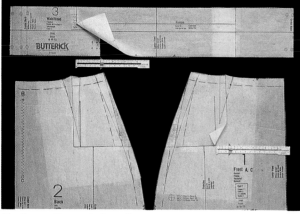

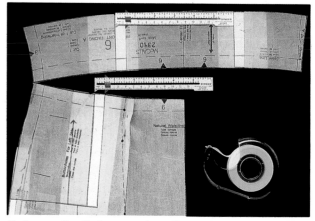

Reduce: On waistband, cut pattern at side seam symbols. On facings, make adjustment at same place as on skirt or pants. *Lap* cut sections to remove the same amount that skirt or pants waist was reduced. Tape cut sections together. Blend stitching and cutting lines.

Enlarge: On facings, make adjustment at same place as on skirt or pants. On waistband, cut pattern at side seam symbols. *Spread* cut sections to add the same amount that skirt or pants waist was enlarged. Tape paper underneath. Blend stitching and cutting lines.

How to Adjust a Bodice Waistline

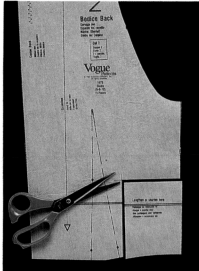

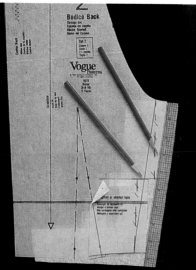

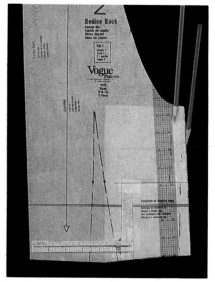

Reduce: 1) Draw adjustment line at side seam halfway between the waistline and underarm, at right angle to grainline. Draw a second line between waistline dart and side seam, parallel to grainline, to connect with the first line. Cut on adjustment lines.

2) Slide adjustment section toward center front until waistline measurement corresponds to skirt waistline. Blend waistline and side seams. It may be necessary to reposition waistline dart (page 74).

Enlarge: Draw and cut adjustment lines as in step 1, left. Slide adjustment section *out* until bodice waistline corresponds to skirt waistline. Tape paper underneath. Blend stitching and cutting lines at waistline and side seams. It may be necessary to reposition waistline dart (page 74).

Waist & Hip Adjustments on Gored Skirts

The many seams of gored skirts simplify waist and hip adjustments, because you are not limited to enlarging or reducing the pattern at the sides. The more gores, or panels, in a skirt pattern, the greater the adjustment that can be made, because small amounts can be added or removed from each seam. If you always require major waist and hip adjustments, skirts with four, six, or more gores are among the best pattern choices.

Minor Waist or Hip Adjustments on Four or Six Gore Skirts

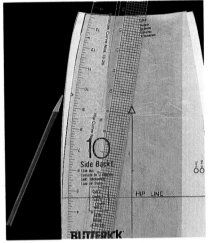

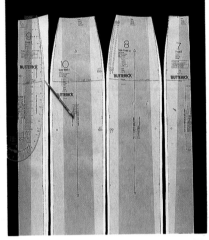

Enlarge: Divide total amount needed by number of seams times two. *Add* up to ⅜" (1 cm) per seam allowance, for total increase of ¾" (2 cm) per seam. Total maximum adjustment for 4-gore skirt is 3" (7.5 cm). Maximum adjustment for 6-gore skirt is 4½" (11.5 cm).

Waist. Add amount at waistline at each seam. Blend stitching and cutting lines to hipline, using curved ruler.

Hips. Mark amount needed to add at hipline (fullest part of hips as measured, page 101). Blend the stitching and cutting lines to the original waistline if enlarging at hips only. Extend hip addition to hem edge.

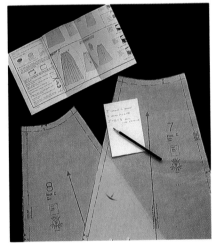

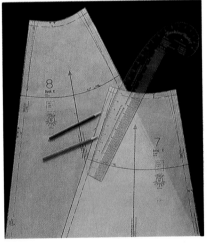

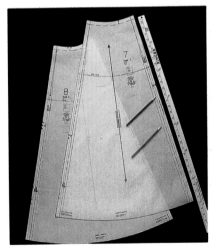

Reduce: Divide total amount of reduction by number of seams times two. *Remove* up to ⅜" (1 cm) per seam allowance, for total reduction of ¾" (2 cm) per seam. Maximum adjustments for 4-gore and 6-gore skirts are same as for enlarging waist or hip, above.

Waist. Mark inside seam allowance the amount needed to reduce. Blend stitching and cutting lines to hipline, using curved ruler.

Hips. Mark the amount needed to reduce at hipline. Blend stitching and cutting lines to original waistline if reducing at hips only. Extend hip reduction to hem edge.

Fitting Hips

When garments fit well at the hipline, they feel comfortable whether you are standing or sitting. They also look smooth, without strained wrinkles or excess fabric folds.

Before adjusting for width, make any basic lengthening or shortening adjustments below the waistline. Length adjustments may eliminate the need for adjusting pattern hip circumference. If you have one hip higher than the other, it may be necessary to make a copy of the pattern and adjust

a separate pattern piece for each side of the body. If your hips are fuller or slimmer than the average, adjust the pattern to include the right amount of ease. For wearing comfort, there must be a minimum of 2" (5 cm) ease, or extra room, at the hipline of the garment for sizes smaller than 16. For size 16 or larger, there must be at least 2½" (6.5 cm) of ease. You may need more than minimum ease for good fit if you have full hips or are using a thick fabric. You may need less if you are working with a knit.

How to Determine Pattern Adjustments

1) Determine where hipline falls by measuring at the side seam from waist to fullest part of hips. Measure hips, keeping tape measure parallel to floor. Add 2" to 2½" (5 to 6.5 cm) minimum ease to measurement.

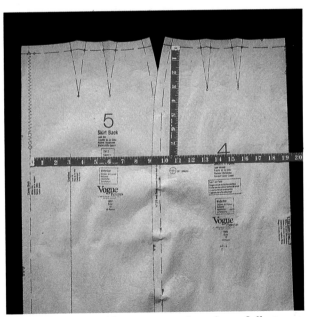

2) Mark pattern side seam at point where fullest part of hipline falls. Lap the back and front pattern pieces at mark. Measure hipline from center front to center back at this position. Double this measurement to arrive at total finished circumference. Compare with hip measurement plus ease to determine if adjustment is needed.

Full Hips

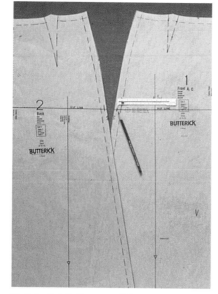

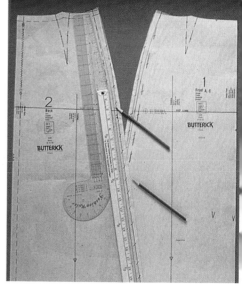

Minor Adjustment

Poor fit causes horizontal wrinkles across hips. Skirt cups under seat in back. Skirt tends to ride up, because there is not enough width at hip level to fit full hips. Pattern needs enlarging at hipline.

1) Mark hipline at side seam of back and front patterns. Add one-fourth the amount needed at each side seam, next to mark. Add maximum of ⅜" (1 cm) per seam allowance for total of ¾" (2 cm) per seam.

2) Blend stitching and cutting lines from hip to waist with curved ruler. Mark new stitching and cutting lines from hip to hem with straight edge.

Small Hips

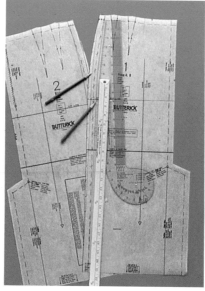

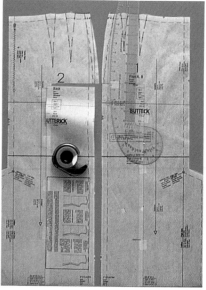

Minor Adjustment

Major Adjustment

Poor fit causes excess fabric to drape in folds and look baggy. Skirt hipline is too broad for figure with slender hips. Pattern width needs reduction at hipline, and darts may have to be reduced.

Mark hipline at side seam on back and front patterns. Remove one-fourth the amount needed at each side seam, next to mark. Remove up to ⅜" (1 cm) per seam allowance for total of ¾" (2 cm) per seam. Mark new stitching and cutting lines as in step 2, above.

Draw adjustment line and cut as for major adjustment for full hips. Slide section *in* to remove one-fourth the amount needed. Remove a maximum of ¾" (2 cm) from sizes under 16 for total of 1½" (3.8 cm) per seam, and 1" (2.5 cm) from sizes 16 and above for total of 2" (5 cm) per seam. Blend stitching and cutting lines from hip to waist with curved ruler.

Major Adjustment

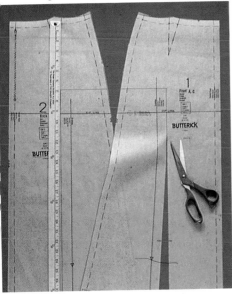

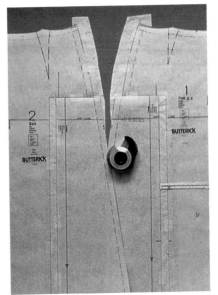

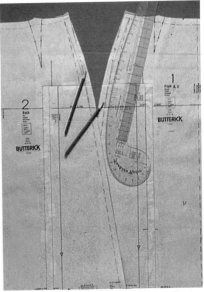

1) Mark hipline next to side seam of back and front patterns. Draw a 4" to 5" (10 to 12.5 cm) adjustment line at side seam at right angle to grainline, 2" to 3" (5 to 7.5 cm) above hip mark. Draw second line parallel to grainline from end of first line to hem. Cut on lines.

2) Slide section *out* to add one-fourth the amount needed. Add maximum of 1" (2.5 cm) to sizes under 16 for total of 2" (5 cm) per seam, and 1½" (3.8 cm) to sizes 16 and above for total of 3" (7.5 cm) per seam.

3) Blend stitching and cutting lines from hip to waist with curved ruler.

One High Hip

How to Adjust Pattern for One High Hip

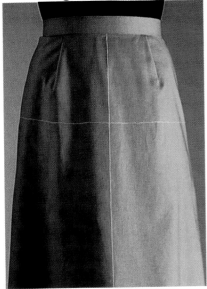

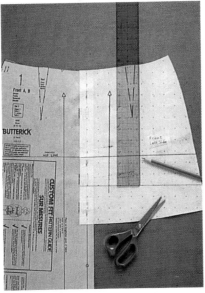

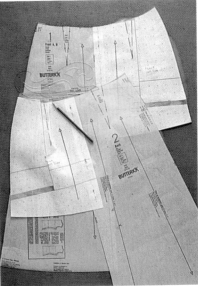

Poor fit causes diagonal wrinkles on one side only. Uneven figure with one high hip pulls fabric off-grain. High hip may be slimmer or fuller than other hip.

1) Trace front and back skirt patterns from 5" (12.5 cm) below hipline. Use traced pattern for high hip side. Draw adjustment line 2" to 3" (5 to 7.5 cm) below marked hipline, at right angle to grainline. Draw second line parallel to grainline through waistline. Cut on adjustment lines.

2) Slide section *up* to add extra length for fitting higher hip or *out* for wider hip. Adjust skirt back and front patterns to match. Tape paper underneath. Blend stitching and cutting lines. Label patterns for right or left side of figure, whichever side has high hip.

Fitting Pants

Pants that fit properly can be flattering to many figures. They should hang straight from hips to hem without sagging, wrinkling, or pulling. Inseams and side seams are straight, without slanting toward the back or the front. The pants should be comfortable when you stand, sit, bend, or walk.

To customize pants fit to your figure, begin with the crotch depth and length adjustments. The *crotch depth* measurement relates to the distance from waist to crotch and is usually adjusted if your torso is longer or shorter than the average figure. The *crotch length* measurement relates to the contours of the lower torso. These adjustments may be made for full or flat seat, full abdomen, or swayback.

If you make waist or hip adjustments for skirts, make the same adjustments on pants patterns. Then make minor thigh width adjustments. After all other adjustments have been made, adjust the pants length. Because one adjustment often combines with another, blend stitching and cutting lines after all adjustments have been completed.

To fine-tune the crotch and seat areas, and to make major thigh width adjustments, you may find it helpful to work with a fabric fitting shell or trial garment. Once you have worked out the fit in the trial garment, you will know which pattern adjustments are necessary. You do not have to make a fitting shell every time you sew unless your figure changes substantially.

Wearing ease is important to comfortable pants. Use less ease if you desire a close jeans fit or wear a small pattern size. Increase the ease for slacks with soft front pleats or for a jumpsuit. Full-figures or large sizes may prefer more ease.

Minimum Ease

Crotch depth	½" (1.3 cm) for sizes 4-10 ¾" (2 cm) for sizes 12-16 1" (2.5 cm) for sizes 18 and over
Crotch length	1" to 2" (2.5 to 5 cm)
Waist	¾" to 1" (2 to 2.5 cm)
Hips	2" to 2½" (5 to 6.5 cm)
Thighs	2" (5 cm)

How to Shorten or Lengthen the Crotch Depth

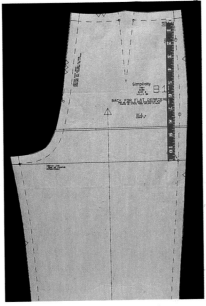

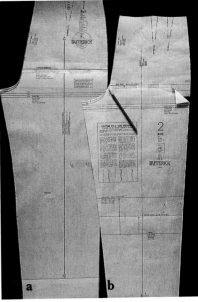

1) Mark waistline with narrow elastic around your waist. Sit on a hard, flat surface with feet flat on floor. Measure side length from waist to surface. This measurement determines pants length above crotch. Add minimum ease from chart above.

2) Compare body measurement plus ease with pattern side length, measuring from waist to crotch line. Most patterns print crotch line on pants back pattern piece. If it is not there, draw it from crotch point to side seam, at right angle to grainline.

3) Cut pattern on adjustment line above crotch if measurements do not agree. Lengthen crotch depth by *spreading* cut edges the total amount of difference (**a**). Shorten crotch depth by *overlapping* cut edges the total amount of difference (**b**). Make matching adjustment on front and back. Blend stitching and cutting lines.

How to Determine Crotch Length Adjustments

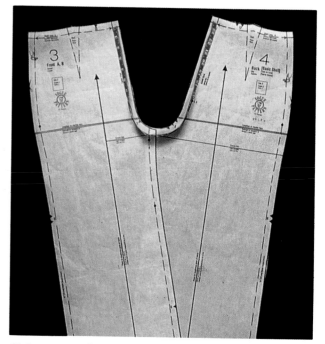

1) Determine waistline location by tying elastic or cord around waist. With tape measure, measure lower torso from center back at waistline to center front waistline. Take snug measurement. Add 1" to 2" (2.5 to 5 cm) ease according to style of pants and personal comfort.

2) Lap pants front and back pattern pieces at point of crotch seam. With tape measure on edge, measure pattern from center back to center front on crotch *stitching* line. Use measurement and figure analysis to determine if adjustments are needed for full abdomen, swayback, or full or flat seat.

Full Abdomen

Minor Adjustment

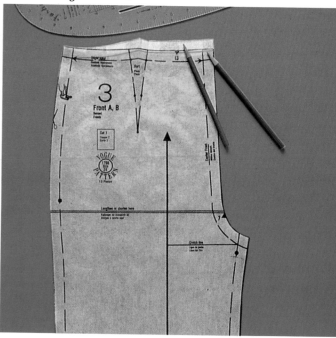

Poor fit causes horizontal wrinkles across lower abdomen and top of legs. Crotch seam feels tight. Front crotch seam is too short for full abdominal contours, so back inseam is pulled forward.

Tape paper underneath waistline of pants front pattern. Extend crotch seam up to ½" (1.3 cm). Raise waist seamline up to ½" (1.3 cm) at center front to add more length. Blend stitching and cutting lines.

Swayback

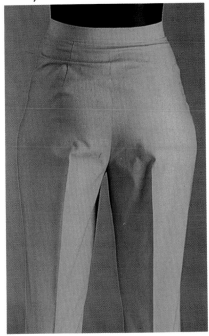

Poor fit is the result of a posture variation that forms a hollow beneath back waist. Wrinkles form at center back because pants are shaped for a figure with more rounded contours.

Adjustment

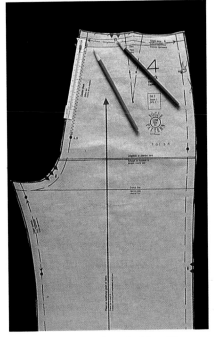

1) Lower the waist stitching line on back pants pattern up to ½" (1.3 cm) for sizes under 16, and up to ¾" (2 cm) for sizes 16 and over. More than ¾" (2 cm) involves other adjustments.

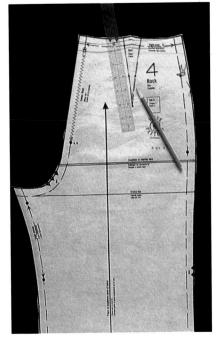

2) Shorten darts (page 51) as needed to fit swayback shape. Blend waist stitching and cutting lines, using curved ruler.

Major Adjustment

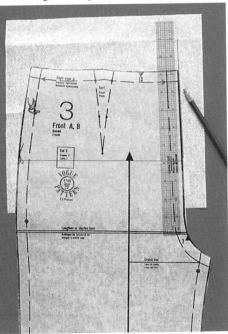

1) Extend crotch seam about 2" (5 cm) above waistline at center front. Draw adjustment line across pattern at fullest part of abdomen, at right angle to grainline.

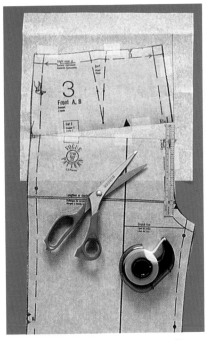

2) Cut pattern on adjustment line from center front to, but not through, side seam. Raise center front the amount needed to correspond to measurement from waistline to inseam.

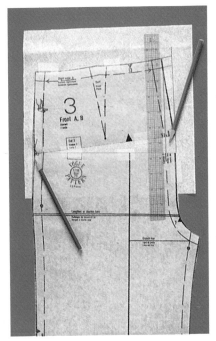

3) Blend stitching and cutting lines from adjustment line to waistline, maintaining original curve. Extend waistline to line at center front. Straighten side seam and adjust darts as necessary.

Full Seat

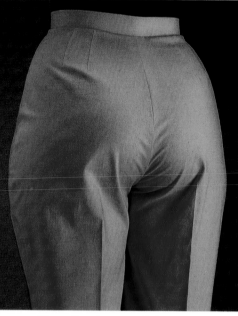

Poor fit creates wrinkles in back. Pants waistline pulls down and inseams pull up to cover full, rounded seat contours. Pants require more back crotch length.

Minor Adjustment

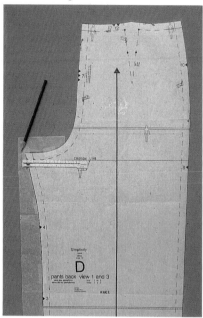

1) Tape paper under crotch curve of back pattern. Extend crotch line to add up to ½" (1.3 cm).

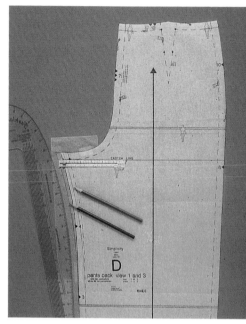

2) Blend stitching and cutting lines at crotch and inseam with curved ruler. Blend inseam stitching and cutting lines to knee with curved ruler. Make adjustment on back pattern only. No adjustment is necessary on pants front.

Flat Seat

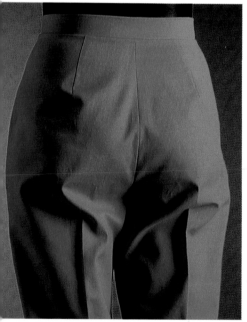

Poor fit creates excess fabric in back. Pants sag below crotch at back of legs because crotch seam is too long for flat seat contours.

Minor Adjustment

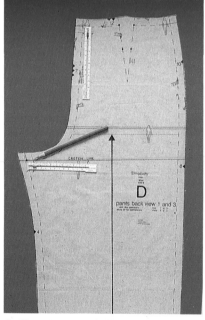

1) Shorten at waistline and crotch extension, removing half the amount needed at each position. Remove up to ½" (1.3 cm) at waistline and crotch line.

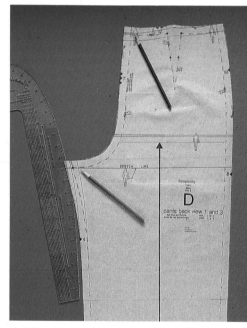

2) Blend stitching and cutting lines at crotch and inseam with curved ruler. Make adjustment on pants back pattern only. No adjustment is necessary on pants front.

Major Adjustment

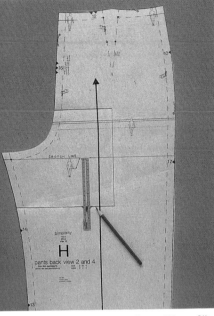

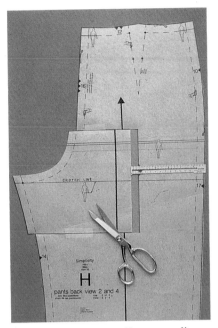

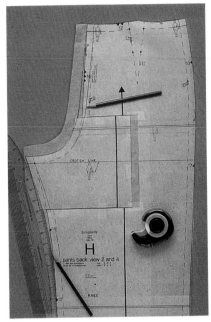

1) Draw adjustment lines 5" to 6" (12.5 to 15 cm) long and 4" (10 cm) above and 4" (10 cm) below crotch line on back pattern, at right angle to grainline. Draw third line parallel to grainline, connecting first two lines.

2) Cut pattern on adjustment lines. Slide crotch section *out* to add the needed amount, keeping crotch line straight. Add up to 1" (2.5 cm) to sizes smaller than 16. Add up to 1½" (3.8 cm) to sizes 16 and larger.

3) Tape paper underneath. Using curved ruler, blend crotch seam up to waistline; blend inseam down to knee. Make adjustments on back pattern only. No adjustments are needed on pants front.

Major Adjustment

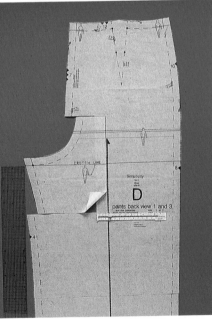

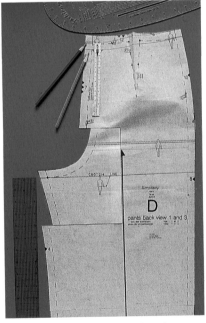

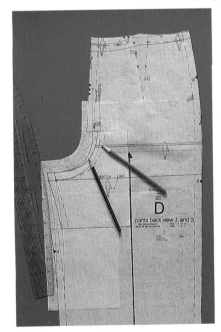

1) Draw adjustment line on pants back pattern as for step 1, above. Cut pattern on adjustment lines. Slide crotch section *in* to shorten crotch seam. Stop adjusting when inseam becomes straight.

2) Shorten up to ½" (1.3 cm) at waistline seam and the balance from crotch extension. Remove up to 1½" (3.8 cm) from sizes smaller than 16. Remove up to 2½" (6.5 cm) from sizes 16 and larger.

3) Blend crotch line *up* to waistline, and inseam *down* to knee. Make adjustment on pants back pattern only. No adjustment is needed on pants front.

How to Determine Thigh Adjustments

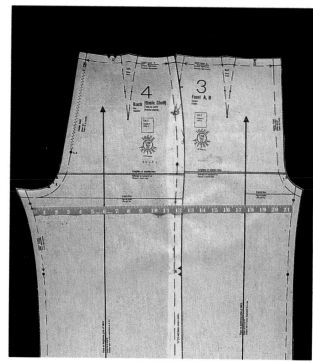

1) Measure thigh around fullest part, and add 2" (5 cm) minimum ease.

2) Lap back and front pants patterns at side seam; pin. Measure thigh circumference at same position on the pattern as measured on the body to determine if width adjustment is needed.

Full Thighs

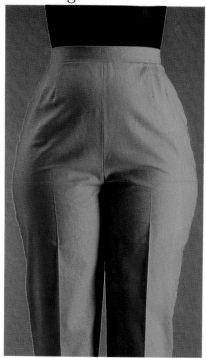

Adjustment

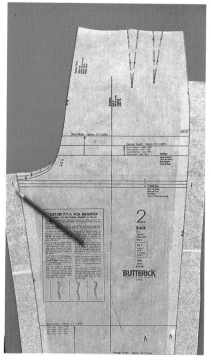

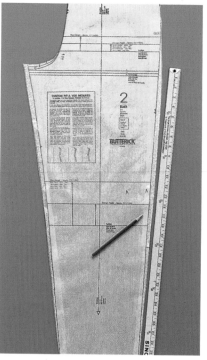

Poor fit causes wrinkles across thigh, at side seams, and across upper inseam. Pants cup under the seat, and front creases are pulled toward the outer seam.

1) Divide total adjustment by four; distribute equal amount between side seams and inseams. Mark amount to be added below crotch line on front and back patterns.

2) Blend side seam adjustments from above hipline to hem; blend inseam adjustments into the crotch seam. Make matching adjustment on back and front.

Full Inner Thighs

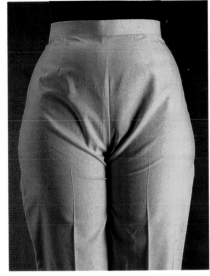

Poor fit causes diagonal wrinkles at inseams. Fabric bunches up to cover full inner thighs, and fabric from the back pulls forward between the legs, causing pants legs to hang off-grain. This problem is often found in combination with full seat.

Adjustment

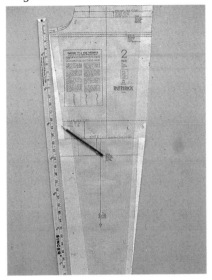

1) Draw adjustment line at knee level, at right angle to grainline. Cut on line; slide lower section toward inseam to add amount needed. Stop adding width when inseam is at right angle to crotch point. Blend side seam from hip to hem; blend inseam from crotch point to hem.

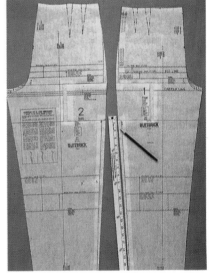

2) Fold adjusted pants pattern in half so inseam matches side seam below knee. Press crease. Unfold and mark a new grainline arrow on the pressed crease. Make matching adjustments on back and front pants pattern pieces.

Full Outer Thighs

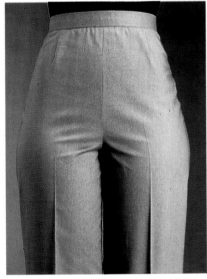

Poor fit causes diagonal wrinkles, because fabric pulls up at side thigh bulges. Pants are not wide enough for full outer thigh contours of the figure.

Adjustment

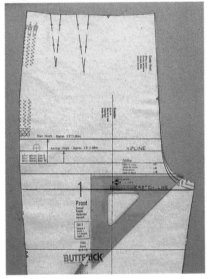

1) Draw adjustment line 1" (2.5 cm) above crotch line, at right angle to the grainline. Draw second line at thigh level, about 4" to 6" (10 to 15 cm) below crotch line, at right angle to grainline. Draw third line parallel to grain, about 1" (2.5 cm) from center of pattern, connecting first two lines.

2) Cut pattern on adjustment lines. Slide section *out* half the amount needed. Add up to ¾" (2 cm) to sizes smaller than 16. Add up to 1" (2.5 cm) to sizes 16 and larger. Blend seamline from above hipline to adjusted side seam at thigh, using curved ruler above crotch line and straight edge from thigh to hemline. Make matching adjustments on front and back.

Thin Thighs

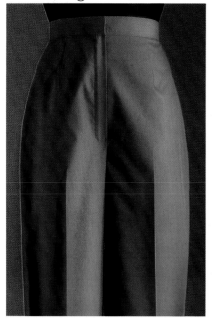

Poor fit occurs when pants bag at thigh, with vertical wrinkles at outseam. On a full figure with thin thighs, pants may also wrinkle at the inseam.

How to Adjust Pattern for Thin Thighs

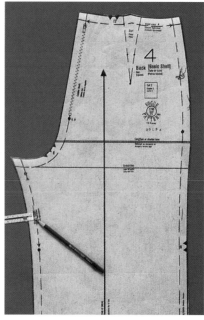

1) Divide total adjustment by four, and distribute between side seams and inseams. Mark amount to be removed below crotch line. Stop reducing pattern thigh width when side seam becomes parallel to grainline arrow.

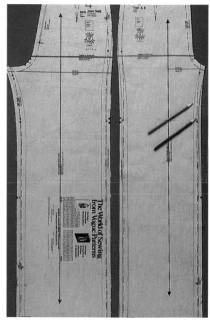

2) Blend side seam adjustments from above hipline to hem; blend inseam adjustments into crotch seam. Make matching adjustments on back and front pattern pieces.

How to Adjust Pants Length

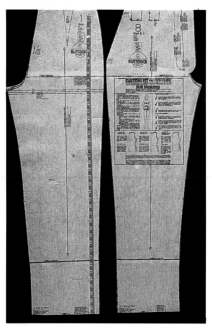

1) Measure finished pants length by standing on 1" (2.5 cm) mark on tape measure and bringing tape measure up to waist. Wear shoes you plan to wear with finished pants. This measurement includes hem allowance.

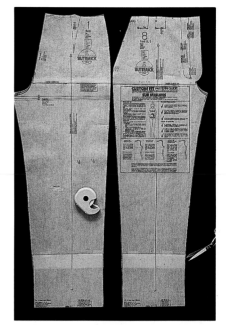

2) Measure length of pants at pattern side seam, after adjusting the crotch depth. Measure from waist to hem cutting line.

3) Lengthen or shorten on lower adjustment line. If pattern has no adjustment line, draw one below knee at right angle to grainline.

Fitting a Trial Pair of Pants

When pants fit involves figure contours at crotch, seat, and thighs, it may be more accurate to determine pattern adjustments by working with a fabric fitting shell or trial garment. Before cutting out the shell, make all adjustments to the pattern as determined by measurements. Use heavy muslin or other firm fabric, adding extra-wide seam allowances to provide room for potential alterations. Use the shell for fitting as on page 53, steps 2 to 4. Note the adjustments to make on future pants patterns.

Adding Wider Seam Allowances for a Fitting Shell

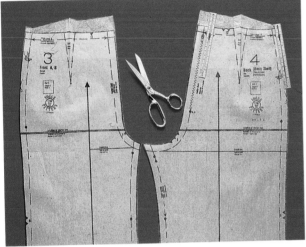

Waist. Cut 1" (2.5 cm) seam allowance on front and back waistline. This provides up to ¾" (2 cm) more length if needed for crotch depth or a hip that is higher on one side than the other. Taper cutting line 2" (5 cm) higher at center front to provide extra room for fitting full abdomen and 2" (5 cm) higher at center back for full seat.

Side seams. Cut 1" (2.5 cm) seam allowances on the front and back side seams. This adds up to ¾" (2 cm) on each side to fit the waist, hips, and outer thighs.

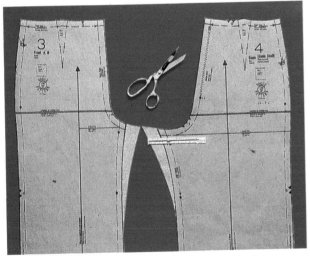

Inseams. Cut 2" (5 cm) seam allowance on front and back inseams at crotch point, tapering back into original seam allowance about 10" (25.5 cm) below crotch. Extra seam width provides up to 3½" (9 cm) per leg to fit heavy inner thighs, or to extend front and back crotch lengths to fit full seat and lower abdominal contours.

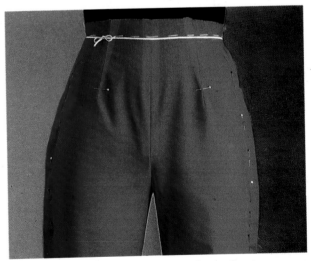

Pin-fit. Machine-baste inseam and crotch seam on original seamline. Pin front to back at side seams with wrong sides together. Try on with pants right side out. Tie narrow elastic at waist, and mark waistline. Pin-fit trial pants, letting out or taking in seams as necessary.

Fine Tuning

The Fine Points of Fit

Professional dressmakers use the fitting session to determine whether any alterations are required before the garment is completed. You can use the same tips and techniques to achieve quality fit in the garments you sew.

To check the fit, try on a garment often while you are sewing. Even if you have made a complete set of pattern adjustments, additional fitting steps may be necessary. It is easier to make them before, rather than after, the last stitch.

A number of minor alterations can be made to fine-tune the garment fit at this point. For example, take in or let out seams a limited amount to correct the ease. Scoop crotch curve or armhole seams slightly to shape them to your figure contours, and add shoulder pads to remove bodice wrinkles.

You can also create figure-flattering optical illusions. For example, you can adjust pleats and gathers, change the way a dart is pressed, or place pockets and buttons to make you look slimmer, taller, or better proportioned. Establishing the most flattering hemline is another fine-fitting point that enhances your total appearance.

Preparing the Garment

Sew shoulder, side, front, and back seams. Pin up hems. Baste set-in sleeves to the bodice, and pin shoulder pads in place. Staystitch necklines and other edges that will be faced. Staystitch waistline seams, but do not apply waistbands. If desired, baste grosgrain ribbon to the waist seamline for fitting. Do not make buttonholes or attach pockets, because you can determine their best placement as you fit. Finish edges and apply these details after fitting.

Before trying on the garment, put on the undergarments and shoes you expect to wear with it. Have any other accessories, such as belts, ready because these, too, can affect garment fit.

To gain the most from a fitting session, ask someone to help. Then stand normally as the helper checks the back and sides, pins in the alterations, and helps you make objective judgments.

How to Alter Waistline Gathers

1) Extend gathering stitches from one side seam to the other, even if gathers are controlled rather than evenly distributed around waistline. Extended stitches allow you to slide the gathers as needed. Do not staystitch waistline before fitting.

2) Try on garment. If skirt is fully gathered around waist, adjust gathers so seams hang straight. Depending on figure contours, this may mean sliding more gathers toward front or back of garment rather than gathering evenly.

3) Slide controlled gathers toward side seams or center front and back as needed to shape garment to figure contours. To minimize contours of full abdomen, slide gathers toward side seams so garment is flat at center front.

How to Redistribute Sleeve Cap Ease

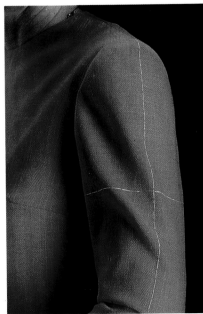

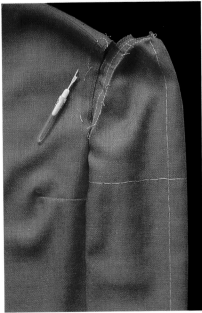

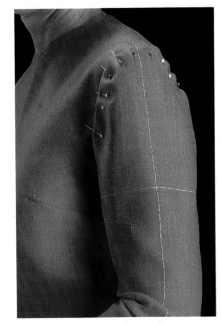

1) Analyze sleeve grainlines to determine whether to rotate sleeve cap toward the front or back of garment. This alteration may be required if you have made shoulder, bust, or upper back adjustments without adjusting sleeve pattern symbols to match.

2) Remove stitches to open sleeve cap seam between notches. Eased area of sleeve cap is between notches. Underarm area does not require altering.

3) Baste sleeve cap into place, redistributing ease to rotate sleeve cap toward front or back of garment as determined in step 1. Before restitching sleeve cap, try on garment to check fit.

Fine Tuning Pleats & Darts

Pleats, darts, tucks, and gathers all are used to shape a garment to the curves of the figure. Although the pattern design may call for one or the other, there are several simple changes that can be made in the fitting process to make them more appropriate to the figure and the fabric. By simply changing the direction of a pleat or tuck, or changing the direction that a dart is pressed, you can create a slimmer or fuller line.

Let out side seams if pleats gape open and pull toward sides. More wearing ease is required for proper garment drape. Let out each seam up to ⅜" (1 cm) to add up to 1½" (3.8 cm) total ease.

When pleats hang properly on one side but are pulled off-grain on the other, one hip may be higher than the other. Let out waistline seam on high hip side only.

Tips for Fine Tuning Pleats

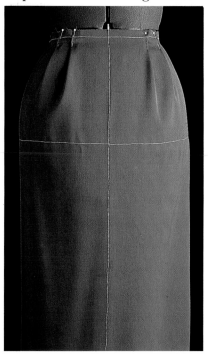

Fold pleats toward side seams to create fuller appearance for flat abdomen. This alteration can help conceal protruding hipbones.

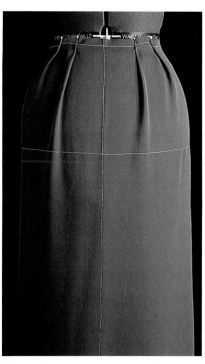

Fold pleats toward center front to create flatter appearance for full abdomen. This alteration can help figure look slimmer.

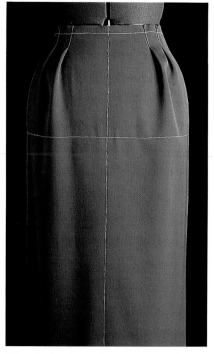

Topstitch pleats for smoother look over full abdomen. When fitting, pin pleats to determine how far below waistline to extend stitching.

Tips for Fine Tuning Darts

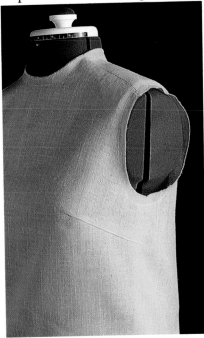

Press bust darts *up* to help create impression of smaller bustline for higher, more youthful look. This is especially recommended for full-busted figures.

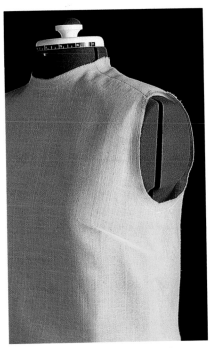

Press bust darts *down* to help create impression of fuller bustline. The two layers of fabric in the folded dart slightly fill out small bust contours, especially if fabric is thick or textured.

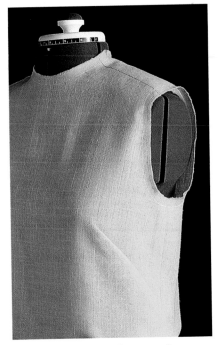

Slant tops of bust darts *up* from the side seam to help create an impression of higher bustline. This alteration is flattering to full-busted figures as well as figures with lower than average bustlines.

Slant waistline darts toward center *front* to help create impression of smaller waistline. This applies to dart fittings for abdomen, hips, or seat as well as for bust. Slant back waistline darts toward center *back*.

Convert waistline darts to gathers to fit flat figure contours of abdomen, hips, or seat. Softer effect fills out flat contours for more attractive image. Use this method on light to mediumweight fabrics that drape well.

Omit waistline darts or reduce dart take-up if figure contours of the abdomen, hips, or seat are flat and the fabric is too crisp for converting darts to gathers. Take in side seams to restore original waistline size.

Fitting with Shoulder Pads

As a fashion accessory, shoulder pads come in and out of style, but they are always appropriate for use as a fitting aid. They offer a quick way to fix many common fitting problems. By adding shoulder pads to a garment, or by using a different shoulder pad thickness from what the pattern calls for, you can often eliminate the need for pattern adjustments and time-consuming garment alterations, as well as camouflage rather than emphasize figure problems. If you have a half-sized figure, or have narrow, sloping shoulders, adding shoulder pads will help make you look trimmer and better balanced than fitting patterns closely to your true figure shape.

Shoulder pads can be purchased in various sizes, shapes, and thicknesses, or you can make your own. Select pad type carefully. Raglan pads cup over your shoulders and shape garments to a soft, rounded shoulder line. Use these pads for garments that have raglan, dolman, or kimono sleeves, and for dropped shoulder styles. Triangular pads sit on top of the shoulders and shape garments to a crisp, squared-off line. Use these pads for garments with set-in sleeves or extended shoulder styles. Insert triangular pads so they extend about ⅜" (1 cm) past the seamline into the sleeve cap.

If a pattern lists shoulder pads as a required notion, do not omit them. Extra room has been added to the shoulder area to accommodate them. Wear the pads for pin-fitting patterns and any garment trial fittings. Do not be afraid to trim the pads or remove some of the filler to customize the pads for better fit. Experiment by pinning the pads in different positions until you find the best permanent location.

When to Add Shoulder Pads

Narrow shoulders. Use shoulder pads to support garment from inside instead of reducing shoulder seam length. Adjusting pattern to fit will emphasize narrowness of shoulders and make figure look bottom-heavy. Shoulder pads camouflage problem for more balanced total image.

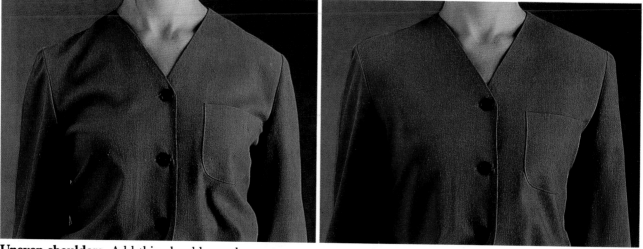

Uneven shoulders. Add thin shoulder pads to garment, increasing filler in pad for lower shoulder to make shoulders look more symmetrical. This eliminates bodice wrinkles beneath lower shoulder.

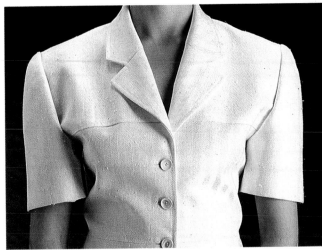

Short waist. Add shoulder pads to lift the bodice of dresses or jumpsuits that are too long for a short-waisted figure. Pads can raise bodice a small amount to bring bust and waist shaping into good position on figure, in some cases eliminating the need for extensive garment alterations.

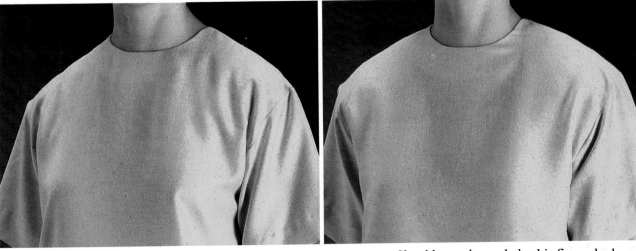

Sloping shoulders. Use shoulder pads to raise garment to average shoulder slope from inside instead of increasing shoulder seam slant of the garment. Shoulder pads can help this figure look more youthful and trim, while eliminating the drooping bodice, which causes wrinkling.

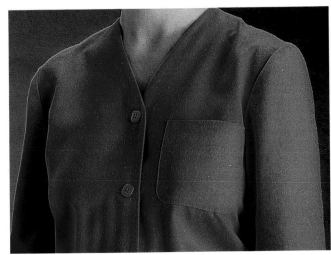

Full bust. Add shoulder pads to lift bodice and eliminate wrinkles that form at armholes. If bust cup is size C or larger, combine shoulder pads with pattern adjustment for full bust.

Scooping Curved Seams

It may become obvious during fitting that curved seams, especially those at armholes and pants crotch, need to be scooped, or stitched deeper, for a better fit. You can make this simple alteration without ripping or rejoining a seam, because the seam can be adjusted after the fitting. Take in the seam a small amount, check the fit, and if necessary, repeat the stitching until the fit is satisfactory. Before altering beyond the recommended amount, check the fit to be sure the altered seam allows for easy movement.

Pants Crotch

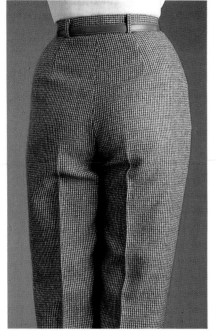

Poor fit. Excess fabric wrinkles at rounded part of seat.

Stitch crotch curve ¼" (6 mm) deeper. Taper stitching back into original front and back seams at notches. Try on pants to check fit. Repeat alteration if necessary. Trim seam allowance.

Altered crotch area after seam has been scooped has no wrinkles.

Set-in Sleeves

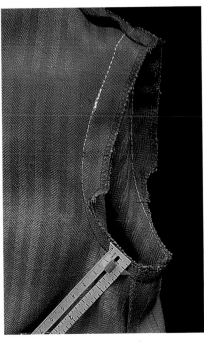

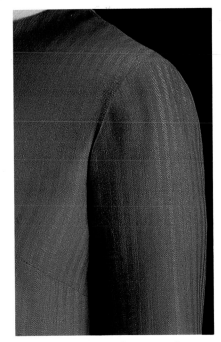

Poor fit. Armhole is too tight.

Stitch underarm area of seam ¼" to ½" (6 mm to 1.3 cm) lower. Taper stitching back into original armhole seam at notches. Stitch again, close to alteration. Trim seam allowance.

Altered armhole after seam has been scooped does not bind.

Dolman Sleeves

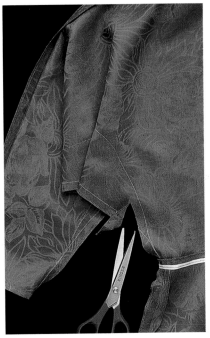

Poor fit. Sleeve has too much fullness for flattering look.

Stitch underarm area of sleeve seam deeper to remove excess fabric. Taper stitching back into original seam at sleeve hem and waist. Trim and clip the seam allowance.

Altered sleeve with scooped seam has the right amount of fullness and does not look baggy.

Flattering Optical Illusions

Fitting involves a total head-to-toe appearance that can help give an impression of a well-proportioned figure. Among the final fitting steps are establishing hemlines, altering waistbands, and selecting your accessories. As you take these steps, you can enhance your image by making your figure appear shorter, taller, fuller, or slimmer.

To create the desired optical illusions, use horizontal or vertical emphasis. Hemlines, waistbands, and belts create a horizontal line. Horizontal lines tend to shorten and broaden the figure. Buttons down the front of a dress create a vertical line. Vertical lines tend to lengthen and slenderize the figure.

Avoid placing hemlines across full figure areas. Hemlines on short sleeves, for example, should fall above the fullest part of the bust. Place jacket hems above or below the fullest part of hips, and skirt hems above or below the fullest part of calves.

Angle hemlines on narrow or straight-leg pants to make the figure seem taller. Taper the hem ¼" to ½" (6 mm to 1.3 cm) longer in back than at side seams so the hem partly covers the heel of the shoe. Drop hemlines on wide-leg pants as close to the floor as possible. The higher the shoe heel, the longer the hemline can be.

Cuffs make legs seem shorter; tapered hemlines make figure seem taller.

Hem short sleeves above or below fullest part of bust.

Bloused top gives illusion of height.

Narrow belts flatter full-busted figures.

Raise the pants hemline until it grazes the top of the foot to make legs appear shorter. Cuffs and narrow waistbands are other ways to minimize leg length.

Tuck tops into skirts and pants; then adjust the top so it blouses over the belt or waistband to create an illusion of greater height for short-waisted figures. Wear belts looser so they ride lower on the hips.

Alter the waistband width. A narrow waistband makes a figure look longer above the waist. A wide waistband makes a figure look longer below the waist. The waistband width can be as narrow as ¾" (2 cm). Use waistband seam allowances to add up to ⅜" (1 cm) in the finished width. For a greater increase in width, adjust the pattern before cutting.

Select a wide belt to cut the overall impression of height. A belt that contrasts with the top and bottom has the greatest impact. A belt matched to the bottom balances a long-waisted figure. A belt matched to the top balances a short-waisted figure.

Select a narrow belt to flatter a full-busted figure. Choose a color that blends with the garment fabric for the most flattering look. Do not emphasize the waist, even if it is slim, because this makes a full bust look even fuller.

Move buttons closer together on double-breasted closings to look slimmer. Two closely spaced vertical lines are more slenderizing than vertical lines spaced farther apart. Make buttonholes up to ½" (1.3 cm) farther from the edge than the pattern specifies.

Make waistband wider for long-waisted figure.

Closely spaced buttons are slenderizing.

Wide belts make figure look shorter.

Index